MEN & GRIEF

*A Guide for Men Surviving the
Death of a Loved One*

*A Resource for Caregivers and Mental
Health Professionals*

CAROL STAUDACHER

NEW HARBINGER PUBLICATIONS, INC.

Grateful acknowledgment is extended for permission to reprint excerpts from the following copyrighted material:

Touching by Ashley Montague. Copyright 1971, 1978, 1986 by Ashley Montague. Reprinted with permission of HarperCollins Publisher.

The Seasons of a Man's LIfe by Daniel J. Levinson. Copyright 1978 by Daniel J. Levinson. Reprinted with permission of Alfred A. Knopf, Incorporated.

"War and the family: the psychology of antigrief" by E. James Lieberman, M.D., published in *Modern Medicine*. Copyright April 1971, by *Modern Medicine*. Reprinted with permisson of Edgell Communications.

The Flying Boy by John Lee, published by Health Communications, Incorporated. Copyright 1987 by John Lee and reprinted with his permission.

How I Committed Suicide by C.L. Sulzberger. Copyright 1982 by C.L. Sulzberger. Reprinted with permission of Houghton Mifflin Company.

Men and Friendship by Stuart Miller. Copyright 1983 by Stuart Miller. Reprinted with permission of Houghton Mifflin Company.

"The Death of a Son" by Albert F. Knight. Copyright 1986 by The New York Times Company and reprinted with their permission.

Copyright acknowledgments continued on page 223

Publisher's Note

This publication is designed to provide accurate and authoritative information in regard to the subject matter covered. It is sold with the understanding that the publisher is not engaged in rendering psychological, financial, legal, or other professional services. If expert assistance or counseling is needed, the services of a competent professional should be sought.

Library of Congress Catalog Card Number: 90-63756

ISBN 0-934986-72-X Paperback
ISBN 0-934986-73-8 Cloth

Copyright © 1991 by Carol Staudacher
New Harbinger Publications, Inc.
5674 Shattuck Avenue
Oakland, CA 94609

All rights reserved
Printed in the United States of America

Edited by Kirk Johnson
Cover design by SHELBY DESIGNS AND ILLUSTRATES

Printed on recycled paper

First Printing May 1991, 5,000 copies
Second Printing July 1991, 5,000 copies
Third Printing December 1992, 3,000 copies

For Dr. Edward Jarvis, healer, friend and poet, who is a vital source
of wholeness and renewal, inspiration and strength
to countless people, myself among them.
and
For all the men who are now grieving the loss of a loved one.

Acknowledgments

I would like to extend my gratitude to the many men whose grief experiences constitute the vital human core of this work. These men gave hours of time and a great deal of emotional energy to lengthy personal interviews during which they provided accounts of their own grief responses and expressed their deepest concerns and needs regarding the loss of their loved ones. They spoke with integrity, giving careful consideration to the scope and depth of their subject, and in so doing they made indispensable and generous contributions which illuminated the grief experience in a most profound way. I feel deeply honored to have had the trust of the men who allowed me to inquire into their minds and hearts. They are Bob Bander, Robert Chapler, Dana Clarke, John Domingo, George Fuller, Arthur Greenslade, Thomas Hickenbottom, Murray S. Kaufman, Chuck Keefe, Steve Knego, Don Marsh, Dean Metcalf, Donald O'Callaghan, Blair Pascoe, Will Penna, Robert Lee Shippin, Dr. Joseph Silverman, Donald Thompson, Dr. Kenneth Thornton, Dan Viña, Jake Wilhelmi, Brian Winkler, Nick Zachreson, Frank Zimmerman and unnamed others who have requested that their contributions remain anonymous, not only within the text but in the acknowledgments as well.

To those in the field of human services who generously gave their time to read and evaluate the final manuscript, I am deeply grateful: Dr. Max Schneider, Medical Director, St. Joseph Hospital; Orange, Calif., Reverend Thom Harshman, Chaplain, Family Recovery Services, St. Joseph Hospital; Dr. E. James Lieberman, Clinical Professor of Psychiatry, George Washington University School of Medicine, Washington D.C.; David Rogoff, Director of Haven Hospice, J.F.K. Medical Center, Edison, New Jersey; Hyman Eisenberg, National President of Parents of Murdered Children and Other Survivors of Homicide Victims, St. Louis, Missouri; Marvin Allen, Director, Austin Men's Center, Austin, Texas.

Several people supplied key resources or provided referrals for interviews. They are Dr. Kenneth R. Thornton, former Chief of the Department of Laboratory Medicine, Greater Victoria Hospital Society, Victoria, British Columbia, and Professor at the

School of Health Information Service, University of Victoria; Dr. Paul Wood, President of the National Council of Alcoholism and Drug Dependence, New York; Dr. Dale Lund, Department of Gerontology, University of Utah; Don Marsh, Chair of Companion Advocacy Committee of Monterey County Aids Project, Monterey, Calif.; Robert Lee Shippen, Veteran's Counselor, Santa Cruz, Calif.; and Alexis Daley, MFCC, Capitola, Calif.

Murray S. Kaufman and Brian Winkler, who conducted all-male grief groups, generously shared their professional insights, opinions, and experiences. Their contributions greatly enriched the material in Chapter 9.

There were several people who played crucial roles in the book's development and I am grateful to each of them. In 1989, Professor Emeritus Howard Slatoff of California State University at Hayward, a longtime colleague and friend, read the first draft of the manuscript. From that point forward he supported the book in several important ways. First, by his unrelenting belief in the value of the work; second, by his constant encouragement and enthusiasm as the book continued to develop; and third, by his practical assistance at several important junctures of the project.

At New Harbinger, two editors played an important role. Dr. Matthew McKay provided input at the second and third stages of manuscript development, redirecting the focus and tone of the book, and contributing suggestions for significant additions to chapters 2 and 8. In the final lap, Kirk Johnson honed the language.

Steve Turner, officer of the National Writers' Union, journalist, and colleague read the manuscript, offered a thoughtful and valuable assessment of the material, was influential in helping me achieve specific editorial aims, and provided many hours of generous and wise counsel throughout the entire process of writing, editing and production.

Patrick Fanning at New Harbinger coordinated the whole project, exercising a wide range of organizational and interpersonal skills to keep the book on track. Gayle Zanca, Production Manager, worked cooperatively and artfully to turn the vision into a reality.

Joan Marsh offered expert information and advice as well as valuable assurance at a critical stage of the project's development.

During the seemingly endless research process, Andy Kincart was of tremendous help tracking down some of the more stubborn references and preparing materials for the files.

Four people literally kept the motors running by providing assistance in the form of equipment, instruction or technical support. Robert Crandall's contribution made it possible to streamline the manuscript preparation process. Debbie Shayne provided step-by-step technical instruction in word processing even though I was a most resistant pupil, and she also served, very generously, as backup technical support. Cathryn Alpert and Marco Alpert helped me troubleshoot (regardless of the hour) and graciously gave their unfailing support.

I wish to extend my deep appreciation to the many friends and loved ones who have understood my total immersion in this book for four years and who have been interested and patient as I discussed, over and over again, my detailed concerns regarding various phases of the research, writing and editing. In addition to individuals already mentioned, others who logged hours of listening are: Dr. Edward Jarvis, Frank and Kathleen Alviso, Susan Faitos, Nik Macioci, Gaël Roziere, Jan Sturtevant, Steve Wiesinger, Jill Ginghofer, Pam Leri, Ann Simonton, and Louise Thornton.

And finally, no one could offer more support and love than my daughter, Susan Staudacher Becker, whose boundless devotion and concern surpass any reasonable human limits. To her husband Dean, who has certainly done more than his share of patient listening, I also extend my appreciation.

Table of Contents

Introduction

Six years ago, late in the evening, I was concluding a three-hour interview with a couple who had survived the loss of their seventeen-year-old son. Tom had died in a dramatic auto accident one winter night on his way to a high school dance. I had been talking with his parents as part of my research for *Beyond Grief: A Guide For Recovering From The Death Of A Loved One.*

As our discussion wound down, the father looked at me rather urgently and said, "Please say something in your book about **men** and grief. Men don't grieve the same way women do." His face conveyed the enforced patience and emotional exhaustion of one who had experienced both tragedy and isolation — that odd, interior kind of isolation that results from having to find one's own way during unique and painful circumstances. Having access to no behavioral precedent that corresponded to grieving the loss of his son, what the bereaved father had suddenly asked was posed not so much as a request, but as a plea.

As I continued the long process of interviewing survivors, I noted that the grief experiences of men and women were, more often than not, remarkably different. When *Beyond Grief* was published in 1987, it included some specific references to men's grief; but those references were, of necessity, placed within a wide-ranging volume of material that guided the readers through several types of losses. In such a context, men's grief-related characteristics and needs appeared to be merely incidental. It was clear that the subject of men and grief not only required a book of its own, it *demanded* a book of its own.

So my exploration of men's grief continued, with increased intensity and in greater depth. The primary goal was to answer two questions: *What are the common grief-related responses of men? And, How can men's grieving be facilitated to enhance their healing process?*

This book is the product of that exploration. The text identifies the major characteristics of men's grief and discusses their origins and contexts. It explores various ways in which men can facilitate the processing of their own grief; it also serves as a resource for mental health professionals, caregivers and loved ones as they assist survivors. Very simply, the material presents the *what, why,* and *how* of men's grief.

But *Men and Grief* is a book that *begins* the process of exploring and discussing male responses and reactions after the death of a loved one. In no way does the material presented here exhaust the entire range of men's grief experiences. Instead, this research starts at the base of men's grief experience and works its way upward, exploring process and possibility.

When any person deals with grief — probably the most profound and prolonged emotional state ever experienced by a human being — the survivor needs to get at grief's core, to make some sense of it and to trust it. Even though his mind and heart may be plagued by loss, the survivor must continue to believe in wholeness and repair.

So it is with these goals and intentions that *Men and Grief* is presented — to offer courage to men who have lost a loved one, with the hope that they may fully process the grief that must precede their healing. It is hoped, too, that the book will aid survivors to achieve a sense of unity and comfort through identification with and exploration into other men's experiences and perspectives.

Equally as important, this work provides insights, coping strategies and nurturing techniques to caregivers and survivors. It is with deep respect, and the hope for a grieving process that transcends cultural dictates, that this material is offered to the grieving man and all those who care for and about him.

Santa Cruz, California 1991

1

The Way Of Grief

*What does a grieving man do? He does whatever
he believes he needs to do to take care of himself.
It may mean that he'll carry his grief as a solitary
burden in his head and his heart for years. It
doesn't have to be that way.*
(GRIEF COUNSELOR)

Whenever a distinction is made, for any reason, between the behavioral responses of men and women, the first reaction usually is, "Oh, are they different? How?" The very title of this book makes such a distinction. It acknowledges that grief is not experienced in the same way by both genders.

Men and Grief focuses on the special aspects of, and ways to deal with men's characteristic responses to grief. But it is important to note that the differences between men's and women's styles of grieving, although apparent, are not the issue here. The central aim of the book's discussion is to illuminate the responses which make possible the successful resolution of *any* survivor's loss, regardless of the survivor's gender.

Simply put, *there is really only one way to grieve.* That way is to go through the core of grief. Only by experiencing the necessary emotional effects of your loved one's death is it possible for you to eventually resolve the loss. If you try to walk around the perimeter of loss, that loss will remain unresolved, and you will be more likely to endure painful emotional, psychological, or physical consequences.

The death of a loved one is a wrenching, painful, and sometimes almost unendurable experience. Both men and women may respond to a loss in ways that block, delay, or distort the grieving process. A successful grief experience allows you to resolve the loss, to integrate the loss into your life, and to go on living, free of grief-related disturbances.

So before focusing on the grief experience of men alone, it is important to take a look at the general scope of grief. What are the components of the successful grief experience? What course must grief follow to allow the survivor — **any survivor** — eventual well-being after the loss of a loved one?

The Successful Grief Experience

The experience of losing a loved one cannot be likened to any other life event. Death brings obvious and profound sadness and yearning, along with a flood of other less obvious reactions such as emptiness, agony, fear, loneliness, and despair. The feelings which well up in the survivor are so powerful and overwhelming that they could not have been anticipated before the loss and, because of this, they could not have been planned for.

As a result, when a loved one dies, you may feel as if every part of your life — emotions, perceptions, actions, thoughts, and physical body — are in a state of disorder. Even the world itself may seem frighteningly unpredictable, unstable, and unmerciful. How long will the painful and overpowering experience continue? What will it involve?

Grief is not a stable thing. It is a process. A wide variety of emotions and conditions make up that total process. But to fully understand the total process it is best not to try to survey it all at once, but to take it apart as much as possible and see how it begins at the time of the loved one's death, progresses forward, and eventually eases into successful resolution of the loss. The survivor goes through three major phases — or reactions — during the grieving process. These are: **Retreating, Working Through,** and **Resolving.** It must be emphasized that these phases are *fluid* and *overlapping*. There is no *sequential set* of well-defined emotions, conditions, reactions, or responses within any phase of the grieving process. There is only a general progression which must take place to achieve a successful resolution

of the loss, and that progression can best be understood by looking at what one can expect in each phase.

Retreating

**Immediately after the death of a loved one, you are likely
to retreat psychologically.** Retreating is a way of temporarily
managing pain and anxiety. During this phase you may experience shock, numbness, and disbelief. You may also feel some
degree of confusion, disorientation, and denial.

During this period it is unlikely that you will fully recognize
the loss. You'll feel "belief" one minute and disbelief the next. It
is a very difficult time during which a survivor grapples with the
fact that *death means permanently gone.*

It must be emphasized that you may not experience all of
these reactions. In fact, as you begin to take care of immediate
responsibilities such as arranging for your loved one's funeral,
you may feel as though you have accepted the finality of your
loss. It is entirely possible that any significant emotional response
to the death may be absent or temporarily suppressed.

Working Through

**The next phase involves confronting, enduring and work-
ing through a wide range of grief responses.** This Working
Through will involve thinking about, talking about, crying about,
and often writing about the reactions and emotions provoked or
unveiled by the death. It will involve exploring what the death
means to you and acknowledging the ways in which the loss has
affected your life. *This is an intense period of disorganization — emotionally, socially, and physically* — during which you may have to
cope with any number of the following responses:

Sadness
Confusion
Despair
A feeling of abandonment
A feeling of powerlessness, loss of control, helplessness
Fear that is specific

Fear that seems to have no origin
Anger at God; anger at the unfairness of the world
Anger toward the self; anger toward the deceased
Guilt for being alive
Guilt for doing or not doing something
Guilt for not being good enough
Guilt for inheriting something
Guilt for feeling relieved
Auditory or visual hallucinations
Depression
Impeded concentration
Poor memory

Each individual survivor will feel some of the conditions and emotions more strongly than others. Sometimes several emotions will be experienced all at once. And frequently emotions such as anger, guilt, or fear are very powerful and consuming one day and subliminal or weak the next.

It is necessary for you to work through these various emotions and reactions in order to successfully resolve the loss. You must endure the traumatic experience of detaching from your loved one; but the emotions that are produced as a result of the death must not be similarly detached. If they are, they become suppressed or repressed. Simply put, suppression means a *conscious inhibition* of an impulse or feeling in which you are aware that you are keeping things under check. Repression means the *rejection from consciousness* of painful or disagreeable ideas, memories, feelings, or impulses. Repressed feelings are not just pushed down; they are denied.

In a grief experience which evolves toward positive resolution, feelings are not repressed, nor are they suppressed to any extreme degree. Instead, you *think* about your loved one, *talk* about your loved one, and *express* or vent your emotions when alone, as well as in interchanges with close friends and relatives.

Your life will undergo a great deal of change throughout the grieving period. Often your control over your own actions, thoughts, and conversation will be diminished; instead, intense sadness and yearning "take over." Along with these various emotional states, you may experience a number of physiological symptoms, with insomnia and digestive problems among the most common. Other typical symptoms which may occur are loss of appetite, exhaustion, heart palpitations, ringing in the ears, dizziness, headaches, dry mouth, constriction in the throat, and muscular pain. Any of these may surface intermittently or simultaneously. Some will be very persistent; others less bothersome.

You may dream that your loved one is still alive, or imagine seeing or talking to the dead loved one, or even hear the person moving about in the house during the day.

The time frame for this sustained period of grief with all of its accompanying symptoms and conditions is not definite nor predictable. Generally, you are likely to experience a noticeable degree of healing between the end of the sixth month and the beginning of the second year. This means that at some point during this time period, a number of the most painful effects of the loss will have lessened.

Resolving

Finally, during the third phase you start to reinvest emotional energy in a different, changed life. **This process involves reorganizing and restructuring. It may include a change in goals and direction or a reinvestment in a new relationship.**

You adjust to the environment in which the loved one is missing and "reenter the world" by investing in activities, people, ideas, and new (or renewed) interests. During this same time period, you will usually experience a sense of having a changed identity. You were a husband; you are now a single man. You were a father; now you are childless. You were a brother; now you are an only child. It must be emphasized that to successfully integrate the loss into your life, it is necessary for you to experience **both** the **Working Through** and the **Resolving** phases. When either of these phases is missing, you will experience a poor outcome. This may mean delayed grief (grief that comes up months or years later), absent grief (the completely absent expressions and feelings of grief), chronic grief (grief that continues as a permanent and painful state of loss and despair), or addictive or otherwise aberrant behavior.

Up to this point, the material has focused on reviewing the successful grief experience of any survivor. Now let's begin to explore the special ways in which the male survivor experiences the three phases of grief.

Comparing The Grief Responses of Men and Women

The grief responses which are discussed here are those of men and women in the Western culture — a category that includes many ethnicities, occupations, ages and religions. As individuals, all of us have been shaped by traditional expectations and conditions to which we've been exposed since birth. For men, perhaps the most prominent and prevailing of these expectations is that they will be the "strong ones" and will not openly express a wide range of feelings. As a result, men will usually experience the three major phases of grief in a way that differs significantly from that of women.

Some men experience a shorter Working Through phase during which the varied emotions and conditions of grief are both realized and expressed. Other men *appear* to go through only the first (Retreating) and third (Resolving) phases of grief. *Appear* is an important qualifier because a survivor cannot actually go through a third phase unless the preceding phase has first been experienced. In such cases, where the middle phase is eliminated, the Working Through period is missing completely. Instead, the survivor is shocked by the loss and then he appears to recover without a period of Working Through. Such a recovery is not possible.

It is generally true that the man who expresses, releases, or completely works through grief is the exception rather than the rule. He is less likely to talk about, cry about, and *appear to others* to think about his loss. He'll probably be reluctant to seek the support of others, either individually or in a group. Instead, he's more apt to assume full responsibility for his bereaved state and depend only upon himself.

In contrast, the typical woman survivor has a more overt period of Working Through. Her grief may *appear* to take longer. But, once again, appearance is often deceptive. Because a woman's grief is usually more evident, it may seem prolonged. The reverse is true. Grief which is repressed or suppressed may take a much longer time; it may, in fact, take a lifetime.

In general, women are more communicative about their loss. They usually exhibit a wider range of emotions than men. They more often seek and accept support in one-to-one relationships or as members of a grief support group. When their grief subsides and they have integrated the loss into their changed lives, they will frequently assume supportive roles for other survivors. They may do this individually, as part of an organization or group, or within the parameters of their occupation.

Very simply put, a man's grief may not **show** and it may **seem** to take a shorter period of time. But the pressures it creates are still there and the grief is real. So where does grief go when it doesn't show? Typically, there are five coping styles:

1. To remain silent.

2. To engage in solitary mourning or "secret" grief.

3. To take physical or legal action.

4. To become immersed in activity.

5. To exhibit addictive behavior.

In the next chapter we'll take a close look at each of these responses to see exactly how each one is manifested and to gain an understanding of its origins.

2

Understanding
Men's Grief Responses

*There were times I wanted to go around and say,
"Hey, world. I'm grieving too. I'm not as strong as
you think I am."*

*Who is supported at the funeral? Someone always
makes sure the woman is supported. Nobody
supports the man. The woman gets all the
attention and the man and the children get very
little, if any, attention. People say to the children,
"Be strong for your mother."*

(FATHER WHOSE TEENAGED SON
WAS KILLED IN AN AUTOMOBILE
ACCIDENT)

After the loss of a loved one, many men have thoughts which
echo those of this surviving father. The reason for such a reaction
is simple. Regardless of who the survivor is or what kind of loss
he suffers, the way he is treated will, with rare exception, differ
from the way in which his women relatives and friends are
treated. This different reaction and treatment on the part of
others — which begins *immediately* after his loved one's death —
serves to motivate and reinforce a man's grief responses.

This points up the fact that the major grief responses which
have been identified with men as a group do not arise mysteri-
ously out of nowhere. They are largely the product of cultural

conditioning and psychological reactions, and to a lesser degree, biological factors. Simply put, a man generally responds to the death of a loved one based on the ways he is *taught* to behave, *expected* to behave, *predisposed* to behave and *physically capable* of behaving.

To understand a man's grief, it is certainly not enough to identify or summarize his major responses to the loss of his loved one. But it is crucial to take a look at the origins of each of his responses and the context in which it occurs.

So while it is helpful for you to be aware of *who, what,* and *how,* it is equally important to know *why.* When you take a look at *why,* then some of the traditional ways in which you may restrict, hide, and direct your grief can be modified and loosened. It is hoped that when your grief is viewed in its total context you will — if you're not already — reach out for the type of family and social support which will allow you to **express grief rather than suppress it, and to experience grief after the loss, rather than delay it** for months, years, decades, or even a lifetime.

Cultural Expectations

First, lets take a look at what our culture expects of men. A man in our society is expected to:

- Be in control.
- Be confident.
- Be more concerned with thinking than feeling.
- Be rational and analytical.
- Be assertive.
- Be courageous.
- Be competitive and rivalrous.
- Accomplish tasks and achieve goals.
- Be knowledgable about how mechanical things work.

- Endure stress without giving up or giving in.
- Express anger.
- Be able to bear pain.
- Be sexually potent.
- Be able to "hold his liquor."
- "Settle down" at an appropriate age to be a devoted husband and father.
- Be a provider.

A man is **not** expected to:

- Lose control over a situation, or lose control of himself.
- Openly cry.
- Be afraid.
- Be dependent.
- Be insecure or anxious.
- Be passive.
- Express loneliness, sadness, or depression.
- Express the need for love or affection.
- Exhibit typically "feminine" characteristics.
- Be playful.
- Touch other men.
- Be impotent (sexually or otherwise).

While these demanding and unrealistic expectations may make daily survival possible, they make the successful resolution of a loss very difficult and, in many cases, downright impossible. Given society's strictures on men, it is remarkable that any man expresses the pain of grief and works through a loss until it is resolved. Male sex role conditioning acts strongly, and in direct opposition to the requirements necessary to grieve a loss. As a man, you are on familiar territory, and capable of your most effective efforts, when you are required to **do** something, **solve** something, **oppose** something, or **bear** something (whether it be physical or emotional weight.)

In response to these expectations, many men spend a great deal of time guarding themselves against what they must not be. Much of your psychological energy may go to repressing or suppressing socially disfavored emotions, needs, and impulses; in short, many of the ways in which you might otherwise wish to act. The more you adhere to the expectations society has about men's behavior, the more you may have to guard against what you really need or want. You may invest a significant amount of energy in *not* being afraid, emotional, vulnerable or in need of affection or security — *all conditions which are directly related to basic and powerful human drives.*

In general, men are encouraged to deal with the loss of a loved one by (1) taking charge, (2) supporting others as they "bear up," and (3) accepting death as a challenge, even a *test* of masculinity. Thus, **death may constitute a double crisis: the loss itself, and the behavioral challenge created by coping with the loss.** The problem becomes how to stay "manly" when human needs and drives call for exhibiting "unmanly" emotions.

Let's take a close look now at some of the grief-related responses that you may have found yourself having. Let's go behind each one to consider its various origins.

Remaining Silent

The majority of men react to the death of a loved one by keeping their thoughts and emotional pain to themselves most, if not all of the time. They appear not to need to communicate about the effects of the death, particularly about their innermost feelings. A man who suffered the loss of his father tells about this typical silent reaction on the fourth anniversary of the death:

> ...we [brothers] still cannot comfort each other. We
> sought our solace alone, in silence, as if there were

something wrong in seeking comfort. We hid openly, in
the shade of a tree, with the support of a stone, in the
shelter of a coffin and the safety of detachment.
Receding from them, I watched as always, from
outside that mysterious triangle of pain and loss and
love while somehow being trapped in it, too.

...even without my father being present the family
continued to act as it generally did, silently watching
my mother display emotion for all of us.

(Fred Wistow, "Goodbye,"
Family Therapy Networker)

Not saying anything, or saying very little, protects you
against vulnerability, or against having to explain feelings that
have been expressed. Being silent is often associated with being
withdrawn, mysterious, or defensive. Unfortunately, if you're not
generally expressive, and are not apt to exhibit overt longing,
yearning, or sadness, you may be perceived by your family or
friends as being uncaring about the death, not having real feelings, or as having "forgotten" your dead loved one.

For example, in the case of parents who have lost a child,
the mother will often talk more about the child who has died.
She may yearn or long for the child very openly. At a certain
stage in her grief she may fear that she will not be able to recall
the specifics of her child's life, behavior, or appearance. To help
restore the missing piece of a fading scene or image, she may feel
a strong need for her husband to join her in parental recollections.
If her implied or overt request is met with silence, body language
that does not encourage discussion, or a change of subject, she
may feel that her husband didn't care or that he didn't love the
child as much as she. Of course, this is very rarely the case.

To see how your silence is encouraged, let's take a look at
the messages that filter through via social responses to bereaved
men. These social responses are the norm, regardless of *who has
died, how much the man loved the person, or how recently his loved
one died.* The death of a man's wife, sister, son, friend, or lover
could have occurred, quite literally, only moments before:

Common Social Responses	*Unspoken Messages*
How is your mother (or sister, wife, or daughter) feeling?	Your feelings will remain unsolicited. If you happen to have any, they are to be unacknowledged, ignored.
How is your wife holding up?	You are holding up. Your wife may or may not "hold up." You don't have that option.
How are the children taking it?	You are taking it "like a man." In fact, you're so in control you're detached enough to accurately assess others' emotions.
Call us if we can do anything to help.	You may call others regarding your loss, providing you have a function you need them to perform. Your conversation with others will be a means to accomplish a task. It will have nothing to do with emotions.

None of these messages encourages you — or even allows you, to communicate your feelings. In the course of a series of interviews with male survivors, 95 percent had not discussed the full depth or scope of their emotions prior to the interview. Many men who grieve *never* discuss their feelings regarding a loss.

The following exchange took place during an interview with Jim, a 48-year-old survivor whose wife had died suddenly, ten years before, of a heart attack.

Interviewer:	Did you talk about your feelings to anyone?
Jim:	No. Never.
Interviewer:	How did you manage that?
Jim:	I really don't think anyone would have understood and I don't think anyone would have cared.

Interviewer:	So you've kept it to yourself for ten years?
Jim:	Yes. And emotionally it was the most devastating thing that ever happened to me.

The verbal and nonverbal messages that you often get from others reinforce the expectation that you will not be vulnerable or anxious, or be afraid, dependent, or insecure. Of course, the reality is that the death of a loved one causes *all* of these reactions in most human beings. Death intensifies vulnerability and creates anxiety, fear, increased dependency, and insecurity.

In some cases, keeping feelings in is so much the name of the game that a man's "silence" extends itself into written communication as well. If you write to another family member or friend about the death, you may find yourself telling when the death happened and how it happened (the cause), but mentioning very little about your emotional response except for some general statement such as: "It was a great shock to all of us." "We miss him terribly." "It was hell." Or "(Somebody else) is taking it real hard."

In a study which involved administering questionnaries to bereaved parents, the researchers reported that they observed a "lack of written comments by fathers compared to mothers. In addition, fathers often failed to answer open-ended questions." Again, keeping it all under wraps means keeping yourself intact and safe.

Of course, the cultural expectations that make silence seem necessary are not just present after a death has occurred. For many men, emotional silence can be a way of life which causes difficulties for them in a wide range of normal circumstances. Lack of communication is often a basis of complaint in couple's therapy: "I don't know what he's thinking" (which often means "I don't know what he's feeling"). "He just listens and doesn't say anything."

While silence can be a psychological defense, researchers have speculated that other factors may be involved as well. Differences in the verbal abilities of male and female children have led some to suggest that biological differences may play a role, while others have theorized that since the principal caretaker for most infants is seldom male, girls may have an advantage in learning early language skills. In either case, as children mature, we tend to expect that female children will be more people-oriented, more social, more expressive of their feelings, and more engaging and solicitous. In one study which dealt with the type of language used by mothers and fathers, it was found that fathers used language more often for commands and orders. They were more direct and less polite than mothers. For boys this kind of role modelling can reinforce a reluctance to talk about thoughts or feelings to their parents as often or as easily as their sisters do.

When scheduling interviews which focused on men's grief experiences, it was far more common for men to cancel the initial appointment by "calling in sick", discovering "another appointment" at the last minute, or by "forgetting." Initially, men were much more reluctant than women to talk about their emotional experience. However, it is crucial to note that of the men who were interviewed regarding the loss of a loved one, 97 percent voluntarily expressed positive feelings about breaking their own partial or total silence to discuss their experiences, emotions and conditions of grief. Particularly significant is the fact that many commented on the relief they felt.

> You're bringing out a lot of things I haven't talked
> about or dealt with in a long time, and it's really nice
> to be going over it all at once because it's really
> refreshing my memory about a lot of things. And
> helping me possibly deal with it. I feel relieved.
> *(38-year-old painter whose father
> died during the son's teenaged years)*

> I was scared when I came in here. I was worried about
> it. Wow. I feel so much better. I've never talked about
> it before. Not to anyone.
> *(39-year-old Vietnam vet)*

While being silent is understandable, the "down side" of this response is that so many men have endured years, even decades of pain as the result of a death without expressing any of it. Even though the situation is changing, particularly with men who no longer feel bound by "macho" stereotypes, *there are far too many men suffering serious, wrenching losses in partial or complete silence.*

This silence is often linked to isolated mourning, which is the second of men's major grief responses.

Engaging in Solitary Mourning or "Secret" Grief

Most men find it easier to mourn alone. For example, you may visit the grave of your loved one by yourself so that you may exhibit your emotions and express your thoughts in solitude. You may even cover up your actual whereabouts or activity by telling others that you are "at a meeting," "having a beer after work" or "going to the store" (or on some other errand) when you are actually going to the cemetery.

> Visiting the grave? For some men it was almost every day, and then gradually it became less. They usually go alone.
>
> *(Facilitator of an all male grief group)*

It's a fact that more men than women visit the gravesite by themselves. Some men go at regular intervals at a specific time. They may select a time of the week or month which allows them a more than usual degree of personal freedom, when they can "let down" and risk the emotional pain that grieving brings. It may be late at night, or after work, or only on Wednesday or Sunday. Whenever it is, the visit takes the form of a private ritual. Many male survivors come to terms with death, accept it, grieve their loss, and work out their feelings by going to the cemetery alone.

> I went and visited his grave two years ago for the first time. I made him a promise that I'd contact his family...I cried for the first time when I went to his grave.
>
> *(Vietnam vet whose best friend died during combat)*

> The grief for my brother lasted longer [than the grief for my friend], much longer. I couldn't complete it, but I think I did when I went to that grave by myself and

I was there awhile and said, "Please forgive me for not being there for you." Because I did love him. I loved him very much.

(60-year-old survivor whose brother and friend died within the same year)

Of the men who go to graves, almost all report talking to the loved one who has died. George Burns' manager reported that Burns visited Gracie Allen's grave once a month. "He'll spend a lot of time just standing there, talking to her, letting her know what's happening in his life."

A senior in high school who was driving the car in which his best friend was killed, went alone, month after month, to the cemetery in the middle of the night. He parked in the dark, cried, talked to his friend, relieved his guilt, and asked forgiveness. A ninety-year-old widower who was mourning the loss of his wife of seventy-two years went to the graveyard and talked to her every day for two to three hours. Regardless of the age of the survivor or the *circumstances* of the death, the solitary cemetery visit serves as an important release.

The survivor who sets up his private method for grief, his solitary ritual, often does so with the belief that by exhibiting his sadness secretely he may spare those around him. He may continue these lone activities for long periods of time, and tell no one. Some men reveal their practice after the fact, or they confide in a "stranger," such as a chance acquaintance, a counselor, or other helping professional.

Several of the cultural expectations for men directly correspond to solitary or secret grief. As a man you are not expected to express loneliness, sadness or depression (unless, of course, you do it in an acceptable artistic context such as in the mournful lyrics of a love song.) You are also not expected to exhibit helplessness or to cry openly.

Any man knows that if he allows his emotions to come pouring out, not only may he be labeled as "unmanly," but as "unstable" as well. Knowing this, he may more readily opt for the labels of "distant," "withdrawn," "secretive," or "unfeeling."

I was sitting out in the yard. I was at Soledad (State Prison). They called my name over the loudspeaker that you could hear all over everywhere and they told me to report to the chaplain's office... And there was no reason for them to call me there...I went into the chaplain's office and sat down and I knew he was going to tell me that somebody died. And he said, "Well, I have to tell you that your mother passed away," and he told me I could call home in the evening. As it was, I had to wait until 9 p.m. that night until it was my turn on the telephone list. Anyway, when he told me, it didn't surprise me. It didn't shock me. I remember this because it was so unusual. I noted myself that there was no emotion...I didn't cry...I just took it like another death in Vietnam. I said to myself, "Well, I don't feel like crying. It's too bad, I'm sad, but..." I thought it was very unusual that I didn't have any emotional feelings. I didn't tell anybody anything when I went back outside. I did what Vietnam vets do. They stuff it...The few people that I was halfway close to I didn't think were close enough that I had to tell them my personal life. They might look at me like, "Wow, how do you feel? Are you going to cry?" And I didn't want to show any emotion and I didn't want anybody to look at me.

(39-year-old Vietnam vet and former prisoner at Soledad State Prison)

I had a feeling I needed help. I was very much a loner. Not because I wanted to be, but because there was nobody around who spoke my language. I kept it all to myself.

(72-year-old engineer who, as an adult, grieved the loss of his father from infancy)

The obvious alternative to expressing emotions openly, to grieving in the presence of your family members or friends, is for you to grieve when you are off by yourself. Grief seems to be safer when conducted in private, or secretly.

Grief tends to be experienced internally and alone. There are a lot of things that men experience alone and

inside. There is an intensity to the emotion even
though it might not be expressed outwardly. Inside, its
dramatic because of that. You can imagine, not being
expressed outwardly, it's going to go inside and it's
going to be *felt* inside.

*(35-year-old men's group facilitator
who suffered the loss of his father)*

In a sensory deprivation experiment in which both men and
women were used as subjects, there were some interesting results
which illustrate a man's need to "keep the lid on." Each of the
male and female subjects was put into a soundproofed room having little or no light, and a monotonous background hum — or
no noise at all. Each subject was monitored while in the room.
When interviewed afterward, the women were more likely to ver-
balize their distress than the men. The men, in fact, persisted in
denying that they had difficulty coping with the torment of sensory deprivation, *even though they had been observed during the
course of the experiment to be moaning and writhing.*
    Men's emotions constitute a challenge because they continu-
ally "interfere" with the traditional concepts of masculinity. This
interference often becomes prominently evident when a man experiences the urge to cry, but cultural conditioning dictates that
he should "bite the bullet" instead. To express emotion verbally,
through his body language (by slumping or shaking), by speaking with a trembling voice, or by actually crying would go
against his conditioning. A male survivor aptly illustrated this
point when he answered the question, "What emotion do you exhibit most often?"

The main emotion that I would *show* is that I'm okay.
That I'm in control, that I'm all right. I don't like
that...but that's the thing that jumps out, that I have to
assure people that everything's all right. And I can
handle it. I don't care for that. I really don't. Because
I'm not comfortable with it, and it's not the truth a lot
of the times because if I were really being honest I
would cry a lot more. I go through periods where I
have a great deal of sorrow in me, but I'm

embarrassed by it. I'm self-conscious about it and have a great deal of difficulty dealing with it.

(52-year-old survivor of brother's death and the death of a friend to AIDS)

Even though there is a slowly growing acceptance — and occasionally, even appreciation — for men who are moved to tears, the fact remains that the man who cries, especially in the presence of others, is the exception rather than the norm.

When a male figure cries, it's news; sometimes it even makes the headlines. Consider, for example, the following news reports which appeared in the "enlightened 80's."

Associated Press: 10/28/86
Boyd in tears following loss

Dennis "Oil Can" Boyd, the forgotten man in Boston's pitching plans, was the odd man out Monday night as the New York Mets beat the Red Sox 8-5 in Game 7 to win the World Series. Boyd, hunched over and visibly shaken in his locker, was crying as teammates tried to console him after the game.

Associated Press 2/19/88
Teary ending to Jansen's dream

In the blink of an eye, Dan Jansen's last chance to hang an Olympic speed skating medal on his sister's memory ended in tears...

...At the starting line he embraced his fiance Canadian speed skater Natalie Grenier, burying his head on her shoulder and sobbing visibly, holding her as if he never wanted to let go.

Associated Press 3/11/88
Prince Charles escapes avalanche; friend killed

An avalanche roared down on Prince Charles's skiing party Thursday, killing a close friend. The future British King was unhurt, but a witness said he trembled and wept as a rescue helicopter arrived...

...Witnesses on the mountain said Charles, Prince of Wales, and heir to the throne, looked distraught after the avalanche buried two of the six people in his party. One said he was weeping...

Notice how ridiculous such reports really are. Think for a moment how very odd it would be for a man, even Prince Charles, to have acted otherwise under the circumstances. What if, for example, the newspaper report had stated: "Witnesses on the mountain said Charles, Prince of Wales, and heir to the throne, looked calm and composed after the avalanche buried two of the six people in his party. One said he was tearless...." The point here is, of course, that in our culture we continue to remark upon, even make news of, actions which are perfectly normal and healthy. The media message in the above and similar reports is that *men are not expected to cry.* And when they do, it's worth writing about and talking about.

It is hardly a wonder that a grieving man seeks solitude before he cries (or *if* he cries). One male survivor spoke for many of his brothers when he put it this way, "It's okay for men to cry, but they should be discreet about it. Public tears are not manly."

It isn't just the media that conveys this message; it is also the family system and the school system. In fact, the idea of being discreet about crying is even reinforced by the very institutions that are the closest to death, such as hospitals and mortuaries.

Following the death of his newborn daughter, a father discussed his grief experience on the telephone with his friend.

> I called Steve.
> "We had a daughter, early," I told him. "We named her Kir. She's dead." And I cried.
> Steve listened. He didn't say much either. But when he did, he asked, "How are you?"
> Strange question. No one else seemed to care. To know. To think that men feel loss as much as women do. But I can hurt, and so few people seem to understand that. Most acquaintances express condolences and then ask, "How is Cynthia taking it?"
> Fine, I guess. She's got me. And her women friends. And her mother. And the sympathy of everyone else in the whole world. Why is there an

assumption that I don't bleed inside? That men don't hurt. We do hurt. We are vulnerable. We do feel. And even if we don't admit it, we tend to resent it when nobody asks. But we try not to show hurt. We have crying rooms down the hall where we can let it out and then "be strong" for those who need us.

Earlier...the physician had pointed to a small room down the hall and told me it was mine if I wanted it. A crying room. A man's fortress of solitude.

(Roger Witherspoon, "Say
Brother," Essence)

In *The Hazards Of Being Male*, author Herb Goldberg writes, "There is something about a male in tears whether as a boy or as a man that offends, causes others to run away and to want to 'do something,' to stop it as soon as possible.... From a male, tears create discomfort at best and occasionally even mild disgust at his inability to 'control himself.' Manliness is still equated with poise and composure in the face of tragedy."

Consequently, men often refer to crying as "breaking down." When relating their grief experiences and they say "I broke down," they mean that they shed tears. It is as if breaking through a casing, they remove the necessary all-too-familiar mask.

Phil lost his father when Phil was 35. He recounts his experience of returning to the family home and walking in his father's garden alone, while waiting for his mother and sister to return. He explains that he "broke down in the garden."

Interviewer:	When you said, "I broke down in the garden," breaking down was crying?
Phil:	Um-hum. That is interesting because I use that term.
Interviewer:	Did it last very long?
Phil:	Well, I was sort of through that phase, or whatever, by the time they got back — realizing that no one was there and I really wanted to just unwind or open up. I walked around the whole garden and

> looked at all the different things and
> certain memories would come back. But
> basically I was moving through
> something and I wanted to go through it.
> So by the time they were back, I was
> sitting on a chair in the yard and felt
> comfortable and composed.

So the need to seek a solitary place, a need for expressing feelings in "secret," and crying alone all have their context. Slightly less obvious perhaps is the context which makes probable the next grief response, for it involves behavior which is not only visible but often invites attention.

Taking Physical and Legal Action

A man who loses a loved one often initiates action or engages in action immediately after the death. This response is most commonly seen among men who are surviving the following types of loss:

- The death of a child

- The accidental death of a loved one

- The murder of a loved one

- A friend's death while serving in the military service

A male survivor may actually solicit a physical challenge, mobilize a search party, or seek revenge for a death (especially if it is a murder). He may file a lawsuit or keep a vigil.

It is important to note that while women survivors may engage in physical or legal action just as energetically and effectively, they do so with less frequency. "I cried," said a young mother after the death of an infant son. "My husband went out and chopped down trees."

In reporting the male and female reactions to miscarriage, Elisabeth K. Herz of George Washington University Medical Center states, "In general, the man tends to be more action-oriented... while women may have to relive the miscarriage over and over again."

A couple whose teenaged son was killed in an accident while on a mountain climbing expedition reported their differences after the death. The mother exhibited emotion. She talked about the death. She cried about it and wrote about it. In contrast, immediately after being notified of the death, the father scheduled a trip to the site of the accident. He wanted to "investigate," take pictures, talk to people. To do this, he first needed to get permission from National Park Headquarters, then charter a plane, and finally, charter a helicopter. In the course of these actions, he confronted numerous obstacles which he had to work hard to overcome. The obstacles constituted a challenge that was all-consuming. After the investigation had exhausted itself, he returned home to begin a long and tedious set of activities which were necessary to complete a "tricky business deal." Eventually, the couple divorced, but the father continued on his course of action which eventually led to addictive behavior.

Hui Tark, whose brother died in a boating accident, kept a vigil beside the lake in which his brother drowned. A newspaper report of the incident describes the survivor's ritual. "He rises every day at dawn, dresses in a black sweatsuit and travels from his home to the reservoir. He doesn't trust the task to the park rangers who have said they look for his brother (to surface) twice a day. The surviving brother purchased binoculars and a telescope to aid in his daily searches and has tried to hire professional scuba divers."

A Vietnam vet described surviving a loss for which he assumed responsibility. As a radio dispatcher, he had not been able to get a helicopter in through heavy artillery fire to save a dying fellow Marine. The survivor's reaction to the death was to ask for combat duty. The death accelerated his need to go out, take action, and endanger himself. "I started asking for combat duty in real vigorous, angry language," he emphasized.

The Need To Exert Control

Endless case studies reflect a man's need to do something after the death, to "take control" of the loss. The action a man takes may very well be all-consuming for an extended period of time.

Why do some men plunge into action? Again, let's consider the cultural expectations. The expectation is that a man will be in control, be assertive, and be courageous. He will not lose control of himself or the situation, nor will he be passive, helpless, or afraid. But when a loved one dies, the survivor — *any survivor* — is affected by the impact of the event; it is an impact that goes far beyond human control. *Death, in fact, usurps control, rendering one helpless.*

This emotional state is reflected in the following journal entry written by a father suffering the loss of his two children, ages 9 and 7, in their flaming home.

> The rest of the day, after I had seen Sheila [his ex-wife], was very difficult: alternating bouts of claustrophobia and agoraphobia, spasms of anxiety and uncontrollable trembling. I felt at the mercy of these changing symptoms: as though I had no willpower, no personality left; reduced to a mere vehicle, an object to which things happened.
>
> (John Tittensor, *Year One*)

While every survivor is rendered helpless by death, a man, more often than a woman, will act in some very overt way against feelings of helplessness. You may find yourself reacting to a death by launching a plan, participating in an investigation or escapade, or filing a lawsuit. By becoming active, pursuing something, mobilizing something, testing yourself, challenging great odds, or suing somebody, you're reacting against the powerful emotions created by the loss. It's as if you're saying, "I won't stand by while a loved one dies. I'll do something. Just watch me." You are proving you haven't lost your ability to make decisions, to be incisive, to produce an act upon the world which has acted upon you and those you love.

This strategy of taking action, this attempt at control, is especially prevalent among men who have lost a child or who are surviving the loss of a loved one due to an accidental death or homicide. Janice Lord, in "Survivor Grief Following A Drunk Driving Crash" (*Death Studies*), emphasizes the importance of the control issue: "Professionals who interface with victim's families from the time the crime is committed throughout early weeks need heightened sensitivity to the victim's need to know and to have a sense of control over what happens to themselves and to the offender."

A man who takes action finds it particularly comforting and supportive to interact with other men (in a legal suit, while on a search party, or while investigating the accidental death or murder of their loved one.)

> Men are very invested in not having fear, the kind that will debilitate them. So they need to surround themselves with supports from other men — that they are okay, they're powerful, omnipotent and nothing can destroy them. That is a very constant common denominator I see with men in general. Without that, they would not be able to fight wars or live life.
> Men are petrified, terrified of being helpless, out of control. If they acknowledge that they are helpless or terrified, they wouldn't be able to function.
> *(Men's group counselor)*

Control is an issue that keeps coming back again and again, and for good reason. The need for you to have control is a belief that is reinforced throughout your entire life — within the family, at school, on television, and in books. In most contexts, you are either expected to be *in* control, or struggling to *gain* control.

> Control, I couldn't let go because I had to be in control of my emotions. I had to be in control of my world and, whenever possible, other people's worlds as well. I had tried to control [my woman friend] through manipulation, education and domination while paying lip service to feminism and equality. I always had to be in control. I could never be late. I couldn't stand to be kept waiting — control in a hundred different ways. If I could just control, or maintain the illusion of control by predicting and programming my existence and environment, I thought I might just have a chance in this world.
> (John Lee, *The Flying Boy,*
> *Healing The Wounded Man)*

Control, aggression and competitive behavior are all linked. As a man, you are expected to exhibit your control by acting aggressively and competitively for promotions, sales, raises, bonuses, contracts, clients, territories, equipment, recognition, scores, ratings, and so on. Traditionally, male activity has been set up in accordance with a clear hierarchy which encourages and supports competitive behavior. The ever-present competition to advance is maximized by the various structures in which men operate. We see it in industry and business, in the armed services, in the government, fraternities, trade organizations, factories, and churches. In contrast, collective work which requires no competition is rare in men's lives.

In addition to cultural influences, many scientists believe that there are predisposing factors for male aggression. Studies have shown men in all human societies, regardless of their cultural conditioning, to be more aggressive than women. It has been proven that aggression can be increased by increasing the level of testosterone (male hormone) levels in men. (The same differences among males are found in other primates.)

Aggression and violence (the most extreme form of the "taking action" response), are continually reflected in our language. Consider these familiar phrases, which cover a wide range of everyday situations.

That's a real *killer*.
It was a *smashing* success.
He was *cut off* from his feelings.
Tell him to *cram* it.
When something goes wrong, he just *stuffs it*.
I wanted to *bust* his ass.
He *pounded* his idea home.

The list could go on and on. Our everyday language supports the importance of being "macho," hard-hitting, and making an impact.

When death renders a man "damaged" and "impotent," he may wish to strike out against that which has crippled his world as he knew it, his immediate world in which he could normally produce change by asserting himself.

Aggression, Anger, and Violence as Grief Substitutes

A father whose two children burned to death in their home articulates this sense of having been damaged, of being rendered impotent. His words speak for many men.

> And there is, too, the strange and frightening suppressed violence you become aware of as a substratum of your grief...the bereaved person looks at the world and sees it going its way as if nothing had happened; as if the loved one had never died, never lived. And no matter how hard he strives to be reasonable, he is filled with an anger that must find its outlet. I'm not sure that mine ever has adequately; and I remember those early months (and it still happens from time to time) how I longed for people to say something thoughtless or insensitive so that I could turn on them, perhaps even attack them physically.
>
> ...In my crazed and somehow *enraged* state I was screaming inwardly for the one thing I could never be granted: to have the world as I had known it restored to me. And at the same time I wanted to destroy the world that had hurt me in this way: my mind kept filling with images of myself tearing at walls, at buildings, at people, destroying, hurting, killing even. Mad, unquestionably; but what alternative was there?
>
> (John Tittensor, *Year One*)

Anger may take quite a commanding role after the loss of a loved one. This is further illustrated in a story told by a Vietnam vet who recounts his actions after attending the funeral of his best friend.

> I did not express grief at the funeral. I felt more anger and rage than I did sorrow or sad. My emotional feelings were more of rage and anger. I went back to my company area after it was all over. I was going to go back to Vietnam...go back and make amends... kill...kill "gooks." The anger was very prominent.

In the most extreme cases anger can provoke violence, such as the beating or murder of someone associated with the death. A stockbroker in New York was shot to death in 1987 in the lobby of his New York City office by a brother who blamed him for their father's death four years prior to the shooting. The 56-year-old brother was arrested and charged with murder.

Parents who suffer the loss of a murdered child undergo excruciating anxiety, endless disappointment and frustration, and persistent agonizing nightmares as well as other forms of severe mental torture which continue after the death, particularly throughout the long and complex processes and procedures made necessary by the criminal justice system. It is not surprising that many of these parents are filled with anger, not only for the loss but for the events which seem to go on endlessly after the loss. The following newspaper account describes a situation typical of those experienced by parental survivors.

> The five-year trial of justice has been so long and slow that Jake Wilhelmi has grown militant. He's no longer just a grieving father. He's an angry man. Wilhelmi's disdain for the system has become so visible that he is now searched for weapons when he enters the courtroom. Wilhelmi vents most of his anger at defense attorneys, claiming they deliberately stall proceedings so witnesses' memories will fade or they will move away and won't be able to be located.
>
> But most of all, Wilhelmi is angry because the defense has twice rejected offers by the prosecution to drop its quest for the death penalty if Crew (the murderer) will tell where Andrade's (his daughter's) body is. More than anything else, Wilhelmi wants to know where his daughter's remains are so he can give her a proper burial.
>
> (Mark Bergstrom, "A father's grief for daughter turns to anger," *Santa Cruz Sentinel*)

Another father of a murder victim "took matters into his own hands." He went to the airport where his daughter's murderer was being transported by law enforcement officers and, while faking a telephone conversation in an airport lobby phone booth, he waited for the prisoner to be brought through the terminal. When the prisoner passed by, accompanied by his guards, the father of the murder victim turned and shot him in the head.

It's interesting to note that more than a few people reading of this incident silently congratulated the bereaved father. At the least, many readers had sympathy for him. It's easy to understand such a reaction. Revenge often seems wholly justified to many. Besides allowing a person to vent hostility, expressing anger reinforces the feeling of being right. It provides justification for one's actions.

Anger also empowers a person. It allows him to dismiss self-doubt and to do something he feels needs to be done.

In the more common and less dramatic cases, anger after the death of a loved one simply consumes energy, creates activity, and occupies thoughts to such an extent that other emotions, such as sadness, yearning, longing and despair, do not come to the surface. The father surviving the loss of his four-year-old boy to leukemia reflected on his own grieving process after the death of his son:

> There's nothing left, but finally just to get mad.
> Especially with men. That's what they do.

You may find yourself staying angry at doctors, the medical profession, your spouse, your other children, the high school, the public transportation system, the pharmacist, the manufacturer of the product that caused the death, at God, or at the world in general. Such anger sets up a barrier, a defense, between yourself and the deeper, more painful feelings of loss. But while you may allow anger to temporarily replace feelings of sadness, it is blocking out grief and preventing you from experiencing the successful resolution of your loss. In addition, just as unsafe expressions of anger increase the likelihood of other unfavorable results, such as accidents and injuries, rage turned toward the self can produce a wide range of physical symptoms which may continue as "residues of grief" for years — even a lifetime.

Becoming Immersed in Activity

Closely-related to the "taking action" response, is the response of "immersion in activity," or keeping constantly "busy." This kind of activity tends to focus on the smaller events in life. While "taking action" almost always relates to the death directly, "becoming immersed in activity" can relate to almost anything and everything. Most commonly, it centers around a man's job or his home.

Preoccupation With Work or Domestic Activity

A man who is surviving the death of a loved one is often very diligent, even obsessive, about occupying his time, and he may fill every waking minute with activity. This differs from the dramatic "taking action" response since this kind of immersion appears to fall within the realm of "normal" activity such as working longer hours, taking more business trips, participating vigorously in chores, and running errands that are related to the upkeep of the household. The survivor may become a fervent workaholic, or display an overly zealous preoccupation with daily domestic maintenance. This mode of behavior often appears to others, as well as to the survivor himself, as scattered or even frenzied activity.

A former *New York Times* reporter described his immersion in work-related activity following the death of this wife:

> I sought consciously to set my mind to forgetting the awful tragedy of her abrupt end, by drowning myself in work and constant travel. I rushed like a madman about the earth, seeing Jimmy Carter in Plains, Georgia, and later in the White House and in Paris; seeing Colonel Qadaffi in a Libyan desert tent, seeing Egypt's President Sadat, Israel's Prime Minister Begin, The Shah of Iran, the president of France, the German Chancellor and numerous other figures; writing, working, doing my best to drown out personal thoughts and heartfelt memories. Yet soon I learned that not only is it untrue that the flesh and the devil can best be escaped by running away, but precisely the same is the case with the spirit and an angel.
>
> (C.L. Sulzberger, *How I Committed Suicide*)

The father of a murder victim explained his behavior as a survivor during the time his daughter's disappearance was being investigated and her murderer pursued.

> I was fortunate in the fact that what helped me keep
> my sanity was two things. And that was having a
> private investigator who immediately went to work
> and started getting me some answers. And the second
> was my own work which was strenuous. It kept my
> mind busy — even though I was thinking about the
> murder as I was working. You have to be totally
> involved in something, or there's just no way you're
> going to cope with it. You've got to be doing
> something. You can't just sit around. I'm running a
> piece of equipment and you become a part of that
> machine and you just do things automatically so it
> frees your thoughts to think of the other [the death.] It
> was good therapy for me. You have to feel as if you're
> accomplishing something. You can't vegetate. You have
> to be *involved*. You have to get answers. You've got to
> *know*.

The immersion response and the response of "taking action" for an extended period of time are two of the major ways by which the emotions that are a necessary part of grief can be suppressed and the middle phase of grief — the Working Through phase — can be denied.

> Their homes had become a symbol of death and
> mourning. A number of men said they used almost
> any excuse to stay late at the store or office. Others
> developed a new pattern — going out for a drink with
> the "boys" after work. Home to them meant hurt, not
> haven.
>
> (Hugh Carter and Paul Glick,
> *Marriage and Divorce: A Social
> and Economic Study*)

It's possible that you'll find yourself becoming immersed in activity of one kind or another. Thrusting the mind and body into constant motion consumes time, energy, and thought. It makes it very difficult for you to have time to grieve, to be occupied with thoughts of the loved one, or to have a space into which the feelings of grief may flood. The more distractions and preoccupations there are, the less likely you are to experience the deepest, most disturbing feelings. It is a way to avoid discomfort. The time-consuming (indeed life-consuming) activities are legitimate and acceptable. Who can criticize you for accomplishing something? That is, after all, what you have always been expected to do.

But this assumption that you will *think* and *do* runs counter to your need to feel. It shuts away emotional experiences. While important parts of yourself are developed in this thinking and doing mode, other important components are neglected and stifled. In addition to immersion in job-related or home-related activity which is a common grief response, a fewer number of men pursue other forms of compulsive behavior. These are risk-taking and immersion in recreational or sports activity.

Risk-taking

A father described the way in which action played a part in his grief after his second child, an infant son, died 45 minutes after he was born.

> On the second day after losing Dax, I flew a
> newspaper assignment with the Air Force
> Reconnaissance Unit through the eye of Hurricane
> Jeanne, some 400 miles out over the Gulf of Mexico,
> and I felt a lot better after rolling around in Death for
> a few hours. Being active — especially if there was
> some risk — compensated in a way for the horror of
> having to watch helplessly while a life I desperately
> wanted was snuffed out. If I kept busy, it would all go
> away. Or at least it wouldn't bother me...But it did.
> There had been nothing I could do about it.
>   (Roger Witherspoon, "Say,
>   Brother," *Essence)*

While this risk-taking was temporary, some male survivors put themselves in continually challenging situations which repeatedly threaten their well-being. A grieving adolescent may shoplift or otherwise invite punishment from authority. A grieving man may become deliberately self-destructive.

> The weekend after the funeral, I drove to Santa Cruz in my car, got drunk and drove back over Highway 17, ran into the guardrail a few times, sideswiped a car going in the same direction, tried to outrun... finally a cop stopped me...I was just trying to blow it, I think, I was drunk and I was in a "fuck it" attitude. I was charged with hit and run, drunk driving, and resisting arrest.
>
> *(Vietnam vet)*

A classic example of ongoing risk-taking behavior as a cover for grief is that of Houdini, the famous escape artist. His mother's death affected his actions to an extreme degree.

> [He spent his life escaping from] straitjackets, all manner of manacles, chains, handcuffs, prison cells, chests, hampers, glass boxes, roll-top desks and even iron boilers. With his arms thoroughly secured he leaped from bridges; suspended head downward by block and tackle he loosened himself from meshes of constricting apparatus. He allowed himself to be chained and buried in six feet of earth, to be locked in steel vaults, to be nailed in huge packing cases. Once, breaking free after an endeavor lasting over an hour, he said: 'The pain, torture, agony, and misery of that struggle will forever live in my mind.' His variations on the escape act were endless, nothing being too bizarre, tedious, or difficult so long as the principles of a constraining force were present.
>
> (Louis Bragman, 'Houdini Escapes from Reality,' *The Psychoanalytic Review*)

As is further noted in Chapter 5, Houdini's escapades reflected a thinly disguised desire for self-destruction.

Recreational or Sports Activity

A sport or recreational activity can substitute for grief by consuming physical energy, time and money so that a great effort is required to continually and fully participate in the recreation. For example, a man may drop out, live on a sailboat, or take up surfing or skin diving. He may take up biking or running, pushing himself to go greater and greater distances each week, setting difficult goals and giving increasing importance to his performance until his recreation or sport has priority over most of his other activities.

Excessive Sexual Activity

A man may seek to "lose himself" by submerging himself in obsessive sexual activity. He may see sex not as a way to express his deepest feelings — which may include loneliness, yearning, longing — but to suppress them. He will remain less vulnerable if he concerns himself with physical release and performance, if he uses sexuality as an escape from the activities which may provoke a variety of grief-related emotional conditions. Such an activity (especially if it involves a series of multiple partners) also serves to quell, temporarily, the need to have control over things, to exert power and to put the very act which produces life (birth) in the place of its opposite — death.

All of these ways of "keeping busy" can help a survivor avoid feeling the pain of loss, the deep, wrenching emotions that follow the death of his loved one. But the more all-consuming the round of activities, the more suppressed are the necessary emotions of grief. As a result, the male survivor death rate is higher. Men have more accidents. Males who repress emotions suffer from a variety of physical symptoms, including higher chloresterol levels, ulcers, higher blood pressure, asthma and backaches. Due to different styles of grieving and communication breakdowns, the divorce rate among bereaved parents is exceptionally high.

Masking Fear

If a man is shutting out, avoiding or delaying grief-related feelings, he will be much less likely to openly express emotions of any sort other than anger, or to exhibit genuine compassion toward others. *Most of all, he will not show fear or insecurity.*

Some interesting research (Sarason, Hill and Lekarcyzk) was done with young males and females in regard to revealing their feelings and admitting to fear or anxiety. In one, it was found that boys concentrated on presenting a favorable front to the researcher, a front that denied the existence of feelings. For example, when boys were asked, "Do you sometimes dream about things you don't like to talk about?" or "When one of your friends won't play with you, do you feel badly?" the boys more frequent response was, "No." As was pointed out, it would be difficult to believe that these responses were true, particularly in answer to the latter question. Almost anyone experiences negative feelings when rejected. In summary, the boys in this study tested higher on a measurement instrument called the Lie and Defensiveness Scale.

Male adults know all too well the torment of being labeled afraid or cowardly. They have grown up with the terms that accuse: cry baby, coward, gutless, wimp, sissy, pansy, mamma's boy, ball-less and so on. There is powerful pressure on the male to appear brave.

As has been previously pointed out, a man in motion, one who is achieving, aspiring, and accomplishing, does not appear to be afraid or uncertain. But the fact remains that death *is* frightening. It eliminates predictability. It says anything can happen at any time. It forces every man to consider his insignificance in the greater scheme of things. It forces every man to face mortality.

Regardless of the external action that is taking place, the inner workings of grief continue in some form even under the best of disguises. The following anecdote, related by Herb Goldberg in *The New Male*, dramatically illustrates the conflict that exists between the human mask and the man who wears it.

> Recently I conducted a marathon therapy group for
> married couples in a small city in the Midwest, where

most of the men still behave in gender-traditional ways. I began by asking each man to write about his feelings, about his life as it was for him, and about his marriage. Five of the eight men insisted that they had *no feelings* inside themselves at all. With assistance, they eventually began to get in touch with their emotions, and it was not hard to understand why they had been blocked. Feelings of frustration, resentment, conflict, loneliness and of not being cared for lay underneath. The men were afraid of these emotions and would not know how to deal with them if they ackowledged them. On the surface, in self protection, all of these men were "macho" — detached, hyperrational, and tough...

In a random sampling of male survivors, each man was asked this question: What do you fear most? One third of the men initially reacted as if they hadn't understood the meaning of the question. Their responses were, "What do you mean?" Or, "What do you mean by *fear*?" Or, incredulously, "What do I *fear*?" Following is a selection of representative answers, ranging from those who completely denied the existence of fear to those who fully acknowledged it.

What do you fear most?

House painter:	I'm not really afraid of anything.
Novelist and poet:	I don't fear much. I'm not a very fearful person.
College professor:	Boy, that's a tough one. Nothing comes to mind instantly...except the IRS (laughter).
Men's group facilitator:	Losing my ability to move independently. Being *controlled*.
Vietnam vet:	Me. Myself. My emotions.
Psychologist:	*Everything.*

Stephen Shapiro, author of *Manhood*, writes about the balance necessary to the "manhood-making process." He states, "We men must take the heroic vow not to live dominated by fear nor to wear a mask of invulnerability. The pretense of strength only blinds us to our true emotions and saps the vital energy we need for the process of overcoming these fears. Only in truly overcoming our fears — rather than pretending that they don't exist — can we taste joy and the capacity for generosity and give true pleasure and comfort to others."

And it would be reasonable to add that only in truly overcoming the fear of vulnerability and losing control can you give expression to your deepest, most heartfelt emotions after the death of your loved one.

3

Recognizing and Assisting
The Alcoholic Survivor

*I didn't know what I felt. I didn't want to know
what I felt. I just got up in the morning and
had my glass of scotch. Then for the rest of the
day, every day, it was just me and the bottle
against the world.*

(50-YEAR-OLD WIDOWER)

When the suppression of emotion continues for an extended period of time, it may result in a pathological grief response. In fact,
grief that is suppressed can lead directly to alcohol misuse among
both men and women survivors, but has a higher incidence
among men. As in the case of the previously discussed compulsive behaviors, the addiction has the purpose of numbing or blot-
ting out painful emotion. The difference between alcoholism and
the other compulsive behaviors discussed in the preceding material — such as workaholism — is that alcoholism is a disease.*

Due to a male survivor's genetic makeup, he may be a
potential alcoholic. When the death of his loved one occurs, he is

---

*[Note: This chapter has been included as a general overview for survivors,
loved ones and those assisting the bereaved so that the link between grief and
alcoholism can be acknowledged and further explored by the reader, if need be.
The information presented here serves only as the briefest of introductions to a
wide-ranging subject which is covered in varying degrees and for a variety of
purposes in a full spectrum of professional literature.]

propelled toward an overindulgence in alcohol through two avenues: (1) emotional conflict (feeling and not wanting to feel), and (2) a biological predispositon to alcoholism. Simply put, an alcoholic's body processes alcohol differently than that of a non-alcoholic.

Alcoholism is more prevalent among widowers than widows, and it appears to be more common among widowers than among other men who are survivors; but, in any case, among the bereaved the disease is certainly not confined to those who have lost their spouses. Men who survive the loss of a child, parent, or lover can also become chemically dependent as they struggle to stifle the sadness, longing, guilt or fear that accompanies a loss.

> Nobody talked about my wife's death. To this day my
> parents haven't, and I see this as a form of their
> alcoholism, the disease. The disease inhibits you: don't
> talk, don't trust, don't say anything. *Don't love.*
> *(A divorced recovering alcoholic)*

As in all numbing behavior, when alcohol is used to cope with grief, then *real* grief — the genuine expression of important emotional reactions — is not possible. Feelings are suppressed by being anesthetized.

And, again, power and control enter into the picture. Alcoholic men (compared to those who are not alcoholic) have lower self-esteem and a severely diminished sense of personal power. When death takes away the man's loved one, he is made even *more* acutely aware of his lack of power. Further, because an alcoholic's self-esteem is directly linked with control, he will feel he is a good person when he is controlling alcohol and a bad person when he is not. This adds to his existing emotional pain, and contributes to the feelings of inferiority from which he is trying desperately to escape.

It is obvious, of course, that the male survivor who becomes dependent upon alcohol commits slow suicide; instead of gradually working through his grief, he works his way toward his own death — cirhossis of the liver being one of the most severe physical disorders with which the chemically dependent survivor must cope.

In *A Savage God: A Study of Suicide,* A. Alvarez points out, "...there is another, perhaps more numerous class of suicide to whom the *idea* of taking their own lives is repugnant. These are the people who will do everything to destroy themselves except admit that that is what they're after; they will, that is, do everything except take the final responsiblity for their actions. Hence all those cases of what Karl Menninger calls 'chronic suicide' — the alcoholics and drug addicts who kill themselves slowly and piecemeal, all the while protesting that they are merely taking the necessary steps to make an intolerable life tolerable."

A person who lives with, or is otherwise interacting with a grieving man who drinks excessively may not be sure how to differentiate between *the survivor who is drinking* and *the survivor who is an alcoholic*. A man may be responding to his grief through the use of numbing alcohol, or he may be an alcoholic who clearly had symptoms of alcoholism before the death of his loved one occurred. To discern which survivors are in the danger category and which are less likely to become addicted (no one who drinks can ever be declared in the permanent safety zone), it helps to take a look at how alcoholism works.

Identifying the Alcoholic Survivor

When people are trying to help an alcoholic survivor, he may feel as if they are trying to take away the only relief he has from his emotional pain and suffering. Usually, he will defend against any kind of dealings with psychology, such as reading about the psychological factors which are associated with alcoholism or going to counseling or for clinical treatment. By avoiding such activities, he doesn't have to confront the basic causes of his alcoholism.

But alcohol is insidious, and it will eventually get the survivor's attention in one way or another because it affects the body, mind, and spirit. The early physical symptoms will often be gastritis or other bowel disorders. At an advanced stage there may be cirrhosis of the liver or cancer of the mouth (which is 17 times more common in the drinking person than in the non-drinking person; and in a drinking and smoking person is 150 times more common). Alcohol increases the incidences of accidents, pancreatic disease, high blood pressure, brain dysfunction (memory defects and organic brain disease), and sexual dysfunction.

When trying to accurately assess the danger signs, there are several general behaviors that may indicate alcoholism. These are a continual increase in tolerance, a loss of control over drinking, frequent physical symptoms, abnormal blood tests, and — if the drinker attempts to stop drinking — there are withdrawal symptoms such as nervousness, irritability, a quickened pulse or erratic heartbeat and trembling hands.

On a daily basis, alcoholic behavior manifests itself in a wide variety of ways. The dependent person drinks more heavily when under pressure, in trouble, or after a disappointment or a quarrel. His capacity for "handling" his liquor will increase. That is, he will be required to consume a higher volume of alcohol before he begins to exhibit changes in behavior. He may have a distorted sense of time, memory problems, or "blackouts" even though he doesn't lose consciousness. He will shun events or activities where alcohol is not available. When he begins drinking, he may seem more hurried to get the first drink than he used to be. He may sneak drinks when he thinks others aren't looking and will assume he is "outsmarting" family or friends. He will, however, feel guilty about it at the same time. He may use some food, spice, mouthwash, or gum in an attempt to mask the smell of alcohol.

As a general rule, an alcoholic man will desire to be treated with the type and degree of indulgence one would extend to a child, and when the man's aggressions are exhibited he expects them to be overlooked. He will often prefer to receive mothering from a woman rather than have a partnership in which emotional and sexual intimacy play a part; sexual interest and actual intimacy are not as important to the alcoholic man as patience, caretaking behavior, and maternal affection. In fact, intense intimacy may be very frightening.

A man who is an alcoholic is always preoccupied. His focus cannot be directed to the development and nurturance of a relationship because at some level and to some degree he is concerned with the satisfaction of his addiction. He may also be clouded and numbed to the extent that he is alienated from himself which, of course, makes true intimacy with anyone else impossible.

Such a survivor usually feels anger and resentment toward those closest to him, but he clings to them all the same. Repressed anger, envy and aggression produce guilt which, in turn, compounds his feelings of inferiority.

At variance with other types of survivors, alcoholic men who are grieving will be much more apt to deny the existence of any anger toward the deceased, but they will acknowledge sadness or hurt. A grief group facilitator at a treatment center pointed out that "Often an alcoholic man learned as a boy that he could not be angry at his alcoholic parent without painful consequences. After that parent's death, the alcoholic *fantasizes* that he has been freed from the bind of having anger and not being able to express it. So as a boy, he could not express anger for fear of retaliation and, as an adult, he continues subconsciously to associate his anger with his dead parent, the result being that he denies the existence of his anger."

Denial is the big umbrella under which all of the alcoholic's behavior thrives. A survivor may be so successful at denial that he continues it in the face of eminent danger or severe illness. As has been pointed out by Dr. Gerald G. May in *Addiction and Grace*, "It is not at all unusual to hear aged alcoholics who have lost jobs, families and homes, and who are now hospitalized with advanced cirhossis of the liver saying, 'Hell no, I've never had any trouble with booze. I can take it or leave it.' "

The Alcoholic's Partner

A person who lives with an alcoholic will have his or her own actions (and concerns) which are directly related to the excessive drinking. To some degree, the family member or companion helps support the addiction. This does not mean the person is not compassionate and loving. In fact, the more sympathetic the person is, the more likely he or she will aid the addiction in some way.

Typically, that family member or friend may engage in one or more of the following behaviors:

1. Worry about how much the other person drinks

2. Have financial problems because of alcohol

3. Feel that the male survivor would stop drinking if he loved the other person (daughter, son, mother, or friend)

4. Think the drinker's behavior is caused by his companions

5. Tell lies to cover up for his drinking

6. Endure the upset of routines or meals being delayed or disrupted.

7. Make threats to get the drinker to stop ("I'll leave you" and so on).

8. Think that something that is said or done will increase the drinking

9. Experience hurt or embarrassment as a result of his behavior

10. Endure upsets and scenes at holidays

11. Refuse invitations because of anxiety about drinking

12. Imagine that if the drinker stopped drinking other problems would be solved

13. Feel angry, confused, or depressed

> (adapted from a self-test, Al-
> Anon Family Group Headquarters)

The Alcoholic's Children

Children of an alcoholic parent are deeply involved as well. One of their responses to their parent's drinking will be to keep "the secret." At the same time, they will feel anger, guilt, confusion, anxiety or depression. Children's behaviors which are typically associated with a parent's alcoholism are:

- Withdrawal from family, peers, or both

- Aggression toward others (verbally or physically)

- Frequent illness with such symptoms as headaches or "stomach aches"

- Accident proneness

- Failure in school or truancy

- Excessive moodiness

- Delinquent behavior such as stealing, or use of alcohol or drugs.

Promoting Sobriety

Usually, when a male survivor is addicted to alcohol, those closest to him will react at first (if not for a very long time) by denying the truth. The alcoholic's family will have a pronounced, compelling need to appear normal to the world.

When the facts of alcoholism can no longer be ignored or endured, the family or friends need to take positive steps to promote sobriety. If alcoholism goes unacknowledged or unrecognized and the alcoholic is not treated, the outlook is dim; in some cases, untreated alcoholism can be more physically devastating than cancer. *But with adequate treatment, alcoholics can enjoy a success rate of 80-85%.* Fortunately, there is no longer the horrendous stigma attached to alcoholic treatment programs and self-help groups. More and more people are finding that they would rather seek treatment than continue on a course which would destroy their lives.

A one-to-one confrontation or intervention with a family member or friend will be less effective than confrontation done, with love, by a "team." This group should be made up of family and friends, perhaps three or four of the closest individuals in the male survivor's life, and a person who has no direct emotional investment in the alcoholic's behavior. The outside person can be a medical or mental health professional or an Al-Anon representative who is familiar with intervention techniques. The most appropriate time for such a discussion with the alcoholic may be immediately following a heavy drinking bout.

A survivor who has slipped into self destruction will, with skilled treatment and continuing support, "come back" one day at a time. Through professional help and personal ongoing support, he will learn how to stand on his own feet, accept responsibility for his actions, regain his lost self respect and reinvest his energy in positive behavioral patterns. Men who have started on the road to recovery often remark about the wide range of emotions they are able to enjoy, the many facets of life they have rediscovered, the strong sense of self-worth that propels them toward new goals. Many say that more than anything they are thankful for having the ability and freedom to love and to experience intimacy without fear.

> All in all the factor of time prevails. Sooner or later, if you keep working and doing everything you can do, and listen to the good advice that is given to you and read all the books, and keep in good health, eat good, get enough rest and enough exercise, and go ahead with your week — in a matter of time, if you're really determined, such as I am, you'll get better. I'm not going to do like a lot of guys do who sit in front of the television set with a case of beer and die.
>
> *(67-year-old widower)*

4

Experiencing Loss During Boyhood and Adolescence

I remember being in the hospital, and my mother was talking to the nurses and her voice was cracking. My mother said, "This is my son, Dick. He's my strong right arm through this." And it was a complete falsehood. I wasn't a strong right arm. It almost humiliated me to be introduced in that way. I wasn't strong. I wasn't the man in the family. I just wanted my dad back.

(35-YEAR-OLD MAN, REFLECTING ON THE LOSS OF HIS FATHER WHEN THE SURVIVOR WAS 12 YEARS OLD)

A boy who loses a loved one has his own unique challenges — emotionally, mentally, socially, and physically. Even at a very young age, a grieving male usually gets the message that he is to be "in control," possibly to stand apart from his sister and mother as he carries out the legacy of being a "little man" or a "strong right arm." As compared to their female counterparts, boys and adolescents have more difficulty expressing sadness and longing because they are likely to associate yearning for a parent's presence with unmasculine behavior.

The degree of emotional display, the manner of grieving, and the daily behaviors of a father or brother are usually distinct from the actions of the female family members who are suffering the same loss. A boy or adolescent responds in accordance to most of the same accepted cultural expectations which affect an adult man who has lost a loved one. Some reactions are apparent, while others are less prominent, even invisible. Most often, the young survivor reacts by doing one or more of the following:

- Withdrawing and stifling emotions
- Substituting anger and aggression for other feelings
- Maintaining silence
- Repressing guilt
- Experiencing confusion

A wide range of symptoms are also common to both boys and girls who have lost a loved one. These include sleeping disturbances (insomnia, nightmares, and night terrors), appetite disturbances, bedwetting, abdominal pain, fidgeting, and restlessness. These symptoms and the reactions listed above are, of course, interrelated.

Withdrawing and Stifling Emotions

When a man describes his boyhood reactions after the loss of his parent or sibling, he'll usually say something similar to this: "I withdrew. I kept everything to myself. I didn't show what I was feeling." When he's reflecting on his loss, the man explains that, as a boy, he stifled his sadness, yearning, and longing, regardless of how strongly his emotions were affecting him. At all times, he struggled to stay within the bounds of the cultural expectations for men's behavior.

> I withdrew my emotions, kept them to myself, cried by myself. Whenever I was alone, I kind of let it out. I didn't really share my true feelings with my friends, my intense grief and sense of loss. I kept it all inside myself. I couldn't deal with it.
>
> *(40-year-old reflecting on his father's death when the survivor was 16)*

> In those days I really didn't know what I was thinking
> or feeling. Up until five years ago, I'd never really
> dealt with my grief. When I was in regular therapy, I
> knew that grief was grief, but I didn't know it was
> anything you could really deal with.
>
> *(40-year-old reflecting on his
> father's death when the survivor
> was 18)*

If, at the time of death, a boy is living in a home where his father, older brother, or other close adult male is present, that man will often serve as a behavioral model during the period of mourning. In a family that is surviving the loss of a mother or child, the son's grieving process is usually modeled after that of his father.

> I think that my father really pulled in and put a wall
> around himself after my sister died. It seemed like
> emotion was just cut off about anything that was
> immediate.
>
> *(40-year-old reflecting on his
> father's grief reaction following the
> death of his daughter)*

When a father doesn't show his grief, the son immediately picks up the cue. He reasons, "This is the way I am to behave." Then the withdrawal or "secret grief" of the father and son sets up a gulf between the male and female members of the family, and creates, as one older sister described it, "an odd, uncomfortable distance."

In the throes of a family loss, adults may perceive a young survivor as being unaffected by the death, even outside the realm of grief, because he is too young to fully understand death. It is true that very young children are not able to grasp the meaning of death, but a child at any age will feel some degree of fear as a result of a death. The fears will differ, depending upon the age of the survivor, his loss, and his particular situation. Some of the most common fears are:

- Fear of losing the other parent or sibling

- Fear that he too will die

- Fear of going to sleep
- Fear of being separated from a parent or sibling
- Fear of being unprotected
- Fear of sharing his feelings with others

If the child's caregiver thinks the child is living his life as usual, or is being "protected" from unhappiness — and all the other feelings that surround unhappiness — the child will take whatever course he can and "tough out" his loss, alone and unassisted.

Substituting Anger and Aggression for Other Feelings

One of the courses a child's grief may follow, is that of anger, or even rage.

> I don't remember the funeral. I don't remember anything else from that time period. My sister tells me that at one point I went completely berserk and was throwing a tantrum, screaming and yelling and blaming everyone for killing him, blaming her for killing him, blaming my mother for killing him.
>
> *(35-year-old reflecting on his father's death when the survivor was 12 years old)*

It's not uncommon for a boy to react to the loss of his parent or sibling by yelling, throwing things, and screaming, as if a tantrum big enough would adequately punish the loved one for dying, or would bring the loved one back to life. Similarly, the adolescent may relieve his stifling sense of loss by channeling his emotional pain into any one of a number of aggressive acts:

- Skipping school
- Fights with siblings
- Name calling
- Destruction of property

- Risk-taking actions

- Drug taking

- Alcohol abuse

All of these behaviors serve to focus the attention of others on the boy. He may receive either care or punishment, but, in any case, he is breaking through the wall of his withdrawal to provoke others to respond to him. In such situations, the boy's grief manifests itself in sparks of fury, not streams of tears. It is far better for his anger to be expressed than inhibited, as long as he does not actually harm anyone in the process. When anger is focused and released, it will dissipate; then healing can begin to take place.

Maintaining Silence

A mother who lost her older son while driving the car in which he and his younger brother Jeremy were passengers told of the young survivor's stifled desire for comfort. "Jeremy kept telling me, 'Nobody cares about me. They'll come up to you and they'll say, "How are you?" but they don't ask me how I am.' " She recalls that she told him, "As long as you say you're okay, then people are going to accept that. If you say, 'I'm really hurting,' then if they can handle it, they'll talk to you about it."

When a boy such as Jeremy does not express any of his grief-related feelings through his conversations or actions, the only avenue that remains for him is silence — silence that is usually coupled with an unexpressed need for comfort. The young survivor may move through the house in despair, careful not to mention his sadness to other family members so that he won't "rock the boat." For example, the adolescent who loses his father is often convinced that he must not mention the death to his mother (or sister or grandmother) because it will increase her sorrow.

> My mother's sorrow was so deep, I didn't discuss it
> [the death] with her. We were all aware of it in the
> house. I mean, it was like we were all carrying around
> a big dark spirit on our shoulders. It was so obvious.

The whole house was just in the darkness. We were all
just sort of occupying space in this house of death
where something was really missing. And we could
feel the withdrawal of energy which we all needed and
loved. Which was gone.

*(40-year-old reflecting on his
father's death during the survivor's
teenage years)*

We never talked about it. I didn't even know there was
anything to talk about. I felt that she...I was looking to
her for comfort or something like that...or love...and I
didn't feel that it was there and I just didn't even
know where to begin.

*(43-year-old reflecting on his
father's death when the survivor
was 18)*

Because his mother's grief usually shows, the son believes
that mentioning the loss will make her grief more severe, when,
in fact, it is more likely that sharing their feelings would be a
relief for both people.

Surprisingly, the most available confidante for the adolescent
survivor is often not a family member, but a girlfriend. The teenager more readily responds to his girlfriend's invitation to talk,
her willingness to listen, her openness, sympathy, compassion,
and affection.

I was going steady with someone at that time. I talked
to her. Luckily, she was one of the most sensitive,
intelligent, wonderful women I'd ever been with —
even up to now. She was very bright, very worldly.
She was very sympathetic. She would not pry, but she
would just see if I needed to talk. She was the perfect
person to be with at that time.

*(40-year-old reflecting on the loss of
his father when the survivor was in
high school)*

I had a girlfriend for about a year then, and we were
pretty close. I could talk to her and she wanted to

hear, and she was really supportive. She seemed to
really care about how I felt, and she cried when it was
sad. She really understood what I was feeling, what I
felt...whereas nobody else would let their guard down.

*(40-year-old who survived the death
of two family members during his
teenage years)*

The man who recalls that "nobody else would let their guard
down" makes an important statement. When the young survivor
sees others "keeping their guard up," he follows their example.
He looks around himself cautiously, warily, to find his models;
then he does his best to emulate their behavior. It often means
repression, and as his grief is repressed, so too is his guilt. It is
the rare survivor who feels no guilt.

Repressing Guilt

With a boy or adolescent, guilt is usually prominent among the
feelings he experiences, even though he may not express it. Four
of the major beliefs which commonly cause his guilt are:

- He believes the death is a punishment to him for misbe-
  having.

- He thinks he may have wished the other person dead.

- He believes he did not love the other person enough.

- He did something "horrible," "mean," "stupid," or "in-
  sensitive" after the death.

There are as many sources of guilt as there are thoughts and
actions, and a survivor can convince himself that he should be
guilty about almost anything, regardless of how irrational the
cause may be. He often suffers from thinking that he did not love
enough or openly enough, or that he did not adequately express
his appreciation or devotion to his loved one before the death.

I felt I should have loved them more before they died
so they would have known I really loved them. I
thought they may have gone to their graves without
the proper respect from their son. I really loved them. I

was just sort of a jerk...was always playing or doing
my own thing. I remember saying to myself that I
should have said, "Gee that was really nice of you to
do that," or "Thank you for those cookies," or
whatever. I didn't say what I should have said. I felt it,
but didn't express it. I'm still that way.

*(55-year-old who was orphaned
at 10)*

I had a friend staying overnight, and my sister came
and woke me up in the wee hours of the morning. She
was crying and she said, "Come on. We've got to go to
the hospital. Dad's real sick." I recall being half asleep
and being real irritated because Dad was ruining the
night. I had my friend sleeping over. I had trouble
with the way I was, later after he died. I felt shame
and it took me quite awhile to forgive myself.

*(35-year-old reflecting on his
behavior when he was 12)*

Survivors are as often guilty about something they did after
the death as about something they did before. In fact, because the
young survivor is seldom informed or prepared about what to
expect, say, or do, he may be very likely to do something that
causes him to feel ashamed.

After we were told that my mother had died, my little
brother was crying and I yelled, "Shut up!" He ran
outside and fell down on the lawn. I kept following
him yelling, "Shut up, shut up!" He was crying for me
too. I didn't know it then. I was scared I would cry.

*(27-year-old survivor whose mother
died when he was 13)*

At the funeral, a close friend of mine, a girl I had
grown up with, tried to hold my hand, and I just
shook it away. It was like I couldn't communicate, like
a reflex. Even to this day it amazes me that I did that,
because it really didn't reflect how I felt. I was aware
of feeling regret after I did it.

*(Survivor whose sister died when
he was 16)*

The day of the funeral for my father, I remember saying something I hated myself for. Somebody said, "Sorry your dad died," and I said something like, "Oh, he was just down to skin and bone anyhow." I hated myself for saying that.

(55-year-old reflecting on his
response when he was 10 years old)

The silence that surrounds male grief doesn't encourage the sharing of the specific memories or perceptions which generate guilt. As a result, too often a child or adolescent may keep the regret and shame to himself indefinitely.

Experiencing Confusion

Anger, guilt, and the suppression of feelings are often accompanied by confusion about the responses or events that occurred before and after his loved one's death. In younger boys, the confusion may be about what death is. A retired widower reflecting on the loss of his father when the survivor was six years old was asked, "What did you think death was?" He answered, "I didn't have any idea. I just knew that he went to heaven. My mother was very religious, and that was the only way of explaining to me what happened to my father." His response is similar to those of many male survivors.

In discussions with men who lost a parent at an early age, it was found that all of them had one or more of these experiences in common.

1. The death was not discussed. Frequently they were just told, "Your father died." The cause of death, the context in which it occurred, and the concern or feelings of others didn't enter into the conversation. The announcement of the death took the form of a notification instead of initiating a dialogue between two people who had lost someone they loved.

2. The boys were not physically comforted by the surviving parent or caretaker.

3. The funeral plans, memorial service, and other activities that were taking place around them were not explained or discussed.

4. They were often sent to their bedrooms, to school, to the house of a relative or neighbor, or just "out of the way."

5. They did not attend the funeral services (and in some cases were entirely unaware of them).

An attorney recalled the experience of coming home for lunch when he was 13 and being told by his mother that his father had died. "I was given a tuna sandwich and sent back to school. It was never mentioned again," he said. "My father had died of a heart attack that morning." When questioned about the lack of communication regarding his father's death, the attorney said, "It wasn't acceptable in our family to show grief." Though his case is extreme, many boys in less restrictive circumstances are also left to figure out the death of a close family member on their own as best as they can.

> I was six years old when my father passed away, and I
> didn't really know much about it. All I knew was the
> end result was bad. I remember my mother driving up
> in a funeral car. I said, "Where are you going, Mom?"
> And she didn't say she was going to a funeral. She
> didn't tell us. She sheltered us.
>
> *(Widower reflecting on the loss of
> his father during the survivor's
> childhood)*

The young survivor frequently grapples in silence with the conflict between *feeling* and *knowing* — the turbulent coexistence of the emotional and the rational. Usually, he tries hard to cling to the rational while feeling emotional.

> I still remember in the days, weeks, after my father's
> death, I still remember this powerful longing to be in
> the driveway in front of our house looking down the
> street shortly after five o'clock and feeling that he has
> to drive up the street like he does every day at this
> time and knowing that he will never do it again. And

how unacceptable that was. How can that be true?
How can this happen? This is my dad. And the tears
would start welling up again...

> *(35-year-old whose father died when*
> *the survivor was 12)*

Coping with Memories, Fantasies and Myths

A man who survives the loss of a loved one during his boyhood
or adolescence will almost certainly have lived for a number of
years with memories of experiences which made a deep impres-
sion on him but were not discussed at the time and, in fact, may
never have been mentioned to others.

> Odors. I remember odors. That's really big in my
> mind. The odors of the treatment my dad had. It was
> a terrible smell.
>
> > *(55-year-old whose father died of*
> > *cancer when the son was 10)*

> I remember being in the car with my dad, just the two
> of us, riding in the car. And he said, "Son, one of these
> days I'm going to die, and you're going to have to just
> get along without me." And I just started blubbering
> and crying, saying, "You're not going to die, Dad. You
> won't ever die. You and me, we're pals." And all this
> kid stuff and just crying.
>
> Why did he do that with me? Was he convinced he
> was going to die, or was this just kind of an untasteful
> thing to do with a kid? And I remember he said,
> "You'll think about me once in a while. You'll
> remember your dad." And I thought "How can you
> suggest I'll just think about you once in a while?
> You're one of the biggest things in my life. I love you
> more than anybody!" It was a painful thing for him to
> do.
>
> > *(35-year-old whose father died*
> > *suddenly when the survivor was 12)*

In addition to memories, the surviving child often has strong fantasies as well. Because a child is often insulated from the realities of the death (by not being present when the loved one dies, not going to the funeral home, or not attending the funeral or memorial service), the survivor may create fantasies which are considerably more disturbing than the actual realities. He may imagine that the dead person took the form of a ghost or a grotesque monster. He may believe that dying itself was a form of torture, or that strange things occurred at the funeral service or cemetery. These images may serve to haunt the child, regardless of his intellectual, rational abilities. The only way to dispel such images is to unveil them through open communication with the caregiver. The discussion should take the form of a gentle and caring investigation into the ways in which the boy's feelings and private beliefs compare to reality.

Positive fantasies are just as prevalent and equally as strong as unpleasant ones. Survivors often report fantasy scenes which reflect the forms of magical thinking, such as imagining that the wrong person was buried, and the parent comes back from a trip (or from a neighbor's house, from the store, or from work) and says the death was a mistake, or that the parent or sibling is rescued by the surviving son or brother and brought back to life.

Alternatively, the fantasy may acknowledge that the lost parent is dead, but remember him or her as being perfect in every way. The survivor sees the dead mother or father as always having been loving, interested, and caring. (Unfortunately, the child may then perceive the surviving parent in an opposite way; that is, the young survivor transfers any "badness" from the relationship he had with the dead parent or sibling onto the parent or sibling who remains.)

Author May Sarton has suggested that "we create myths of our lives in order to lead them." To a great extent, the surviving child often creates a myth of his life in order to continue.

> I have a mythology about my father. My sisters can tell
> me things, things he did or said that they recall —
> being abusive or being violent or rude or insensitive.
> It's not that I doubt what they're saying. It's just that it
> doesn't fit into my personal mythology of my father.
>   There is something fairytale-like about his death.
> He went at the perfect time in some ways. He went

when he was still my hero and he was just teetering there. It had begun to happen already, the earliest stages of me breaking away from him. Had he been around for a few more years, we would have wound up bitter enemies. He wouldn't have been my hero. He wouldn't have been dad who picks you up and puts you on his shoulders and walks with you and tells you what a great guy you are.

(35-year-old male whose father died when the boy was in the 8th grade)

After a parent's death, and particularly after the death of a father, many boys create myths of one kind or another. They create a version of the dead parent which is especially idealistic or comforting to them in some special way. Their version of the parent's behavior and characteristics may bear little or no resemblance to the parent as he or she was in real life. Generally though, an elaborate or bizarre myth or fantasy is not a cause for alarm unless the myth is frightening and disturbing, or goes on for too long. A fantasy should wane considerably six to twelve months following the death. If it continues for an extended period of time, counseling can help the survivor to accept the more realistic thoughts and actions which will make it possible for him to resolve his loss.

The Special Issues of Sibling Loss

An additional set of special issues are more exclusively related to surviving the loss of a brother or sister. Specifically, the surviving sibling may experience:

- A changed position within his family

- Anger toward his parents for not preventing the death

- Anger toward his parents for not disclosing the severity of his sibling's condition

- An acute awareness of his own mortality

- Guilt for having hostile wishes toward his sibling

- Guilt for being alive

- Diminished self-esteem as a result of being compared to his sibling

- Resentment toward his sibling whose death resulted from illness

- Specific reactions which result from the loss of his brother or sister to leukemia

A changed position within his family. As a result of his sibling's death, the survivor may become an only child or assume a different role within the family structure. For example, a boy who was a middle child may now be the oldest child. Such a change alters the way in which other family members relate to the survivor. If he has become the oldest as a result of his sibling's death, he may be expected to set an example or to assume the role of caregiver when the parents are absent.

Anger toward his parents for not preventing the death. The young survivor may think that his parents did not provide ample protection or appropriate care for his sibling and, because of this, view his mother and father differently after the death. He sees his parents as lacking the power he had once attributed to them. They become diminished in his eyes. As a result, he may now feel more at risk himself, or he may even believe that if he had been the parent he could have done things much differently and prevented his sibling's death.

Anger towards his parents for not disclosing the severity of his sibling's condition. Specific circumstances may cause the survivor to feel deep-seated, ongoing hostility and anger. For example, parents may try to shield a child by hiding the reality of his sibling's death, or the inevitability of the death. In such cases, the child will only be confused about the parents' motivations or resentful and angry about not being told the truth. As a result, loving and well-meaning parents who are only trying to protect their surviving child may create resentment and anger which can continue for years.

One such case is that of Ted, a physician's son, whose sister died when Ted was 16. Ted's parents kept his sister's terminal condition a secret from him for four years. He was told the truth — that his sister was dying of Hodgkin's Disease — one month prior to her death. He explained his anger at having been deceived:

They lost me, too. I felt so far from them, so out of the picture in every way, shape, and form. I was really angry at my parents, incredibly angry at my parents, for dragging me through that whole thing for four years. They knew what was happening to her. My dad was a doctor and he was sort of overseeing everything. He told a lie to everybody about what was happening to her because you couldn't hide the physical manifestations of the disease. The story was that she had a case of mononucleosis that was a little out of control, wasn't being typical.

My parents were heartbroken and incredibly crushed by it, and I saw this in them. I knew they were experiencing some terrible thing, that they were unhappy. And they never told me that there was anything wrong with her, and I assumed that it was me, that I was doing something wrong. So I spent four years thinking I was a real bad person. It seemed that whatever I did do was not right. It didn't seem they had the proper appreciation for the things I did, successes and little things...or gave the right support. In retrospect, it's easy to see now that they were preoccupied with my sister and this is why I was so terribly angry with them. And still am to this day. I have all the feelings of anger, so that's why I really didn't feel close to them.

This is an extreme example of well-intentioned but desperate and harmful deception. Unfortunately, there are many other forms of deception each of which has its own powerful and lasting effects on the survivor.

An acute awareness of his own mortality. After the loss of any loved one, the survivor experiences a heightened awareness of his own mortality. This reaction is even more pronounced in a child who has lost his sibling. The young survivor has gone through the painful experience of permanent loss and may even have witnessed, first-hand, the actual death of his brother or sister. As a result, he'll be fully aware that his own death could occur at any time. Death is no longer an alien event, but one which is entirely believable and possible.

If the surviving brother is younger than the sibling who died, the brother will anticipate reaching the same age of the sibling at the time of his or her death. That particular birthday becomes an important milestone for the survivor, and he feels relief when his own age surpasses that of his deceased brother or sister. Only then does he know that he has made it through the "danger period."

Guilt for having hostile wishes toward his sibling. There are certainly very few siblings who do not, at one time or another, have hostile feelings or wishes toward one another; but these wishes (or more overt hostile acts) can have serious consequences for the survivor. The boy or adolescent who wishes misfortune or even death upon a brother or sister who dies may firmly believe that he caused the death.

Because a child is by nature egocentric, he thinks that it is possible for his thoughts to produce external events. In such cases, the young survivor does not make any distinction between the wish and the deed. In addition to guilt feelings, the boy may also live with the expectation that he will have to endure some retribution in the future.

Guilt for being alive. A survivor may see death as a kind of exchange. He believes that one life can be substituted for another. He thinks he is living at the expense of the dead sibling, and that the parents preferrred the sibling to the surviving child. The mother of a teenaged boy whose older brother was killed in an auto accident said, "He thinks his father would be happy if he were dead and the other child were still alive. He says it. He thinks the family would prefer his brother's life to his."

In situations like this, the adolescent survivor may begin to emulate his dead brother. He may seek to develop his brother's talents and skills, assume his characteristics, dress similarly, eat the same foods, or even pursue his dead brother's career goals. In these ways, the survivor hopes to keep his brother alive for himself as well as for others. He tries to perpetuate what his brother was in the world.

Usually such identification with the dead loved one is temporary and will gradually dissipate. But if it persists and is carried to such an extreme that he is unable to maintain a separate identity or to develop independently, then professional counseling is recommended.

Diminished self-esteem as a result of being compared to his sibling. In some families, the surviving boy or adolescent may suffer from being compared to his dead brother or sister. If the parents frequently remark on the similarities or differences between the deceased child and the surviving child, the survivor will be acutely aware of the need to "match up."

Because it will be impossible for him to be the other person, he'll devalue the person he really is. His defective self-image will cause problems in many areas, but especially in his relationships with others and in his school performance.

Resentment toward his sibling whose death resulted from illness. It is not unusual for a sibling to feel envious and jealous of a brother or sister who is terminally ill. For months or even years, he may witness his parents directing the major portion of their time, concern, and emotional energy to the ill child. He may be a lonely, envious onlooker as the other child receives praise, privileges, physical affection, and material things which he does not receive. As a result, the young survivor harbors resentment toward the sibling and feels as if the ill brother or sister is purposely robbing him of nurturance and admiration which he dearly wants and needs.

After the death of his brother or sister, the young survivor will still be attempting to cope with the various ways in which the family had directed its energies to the dying child. He may see no way of regaining the affection and attention he wants for his own. In fact, he may have looked forward to being in the spotlight after his sibling's death only to find that he continues to feel neglected and shut out as the parents turn to each other in their grief.

Specific reactions which result from the loss of his brother or sister to leukemia. There is some clinical evidence to suggest that the survivor of a sibling's death to leukemia will experience difficulty in a number of ways. He may be prone to headaches, fear school, refuse to attend school, be a low achiever, exhibit severe anxiety, be depressed, or suffer from abdominal pain. Such a surviving child would be greatly helped by attending a grief support group of his peers and getting professional counseling to help him resolve his grief.

Reentering Society

Shortly after his loved one's death, a young survivor is expected to return to his outside life — his school, sports, extra curricular activities, or job. But a number of important emotional factors may work against his "reentry" into his old routines and environment:

- He may now feel changed or hopelessly different from his peers. He may feel as if he is outside the mainstream, beyond the understanding or care of other people.

- The male who survives the loss of a parent may have to move from his familiar surroundings, his neighborhood or school. If so, he will have to make his reentry on unfamiliar territory. Such a situation greatly increases his insecurity, sense of isolation, and loneliness.

- He may perceive his grief as a constant challenge to be overcome, something to get under his control, rather than experience. This challenge may consume his energy, making him appear distracted, disinterested, and lacking in ability.

- When students return to elementary or high school after a death in the family, usually the death is not readily acknowledged by friends or teachers. The survivor's well-being is not solicited; his true feelings and situation are often ignored. While some classmates or faculty may express condolences, the majority are likely to go on as if nothing has happened. Many people believe that by ignoring a death they are performing an act of kindness.

Three men who lost their fathers during their boyhood or adolescence recalled these reactions:

Dick: I became more withdrawn. Very unsocial, which was not me at all because I was very social in high school, popular...up to that point. I stayed home more and was having emotional problems with not having a dad.

Geoff: I think it left me very insecure. We moved from one place to another and I was always the new kid in school. All the other kids had established their relationships. I went to about ten grammar schools. I was always the strange kid. I didn't establish any friendships. I always felt alone.

Matthew: I remember in eighth grade going back and feeling very isolated. None of my old pals felt like my old pals anymore. There was a vague memory of being sort of challenged.

An early loss may have wide-ranging effects on an adult survivor, depending on a variety of factors which include (1) the number of losses he sustained during his life, (2) how he dealt with his grief in the earlier losses, and (3) the amount and type of support that was available to him. If the death of a loved one was unresolved during a man's boyhood or adolescence, the man will have even more difficulty with the grief-related emotions and conditions which he experiences as an adult. Unresolved or inhibited grief doesn't miraculously disappear when one gets older. It accumulates or finds destructive channels. The adult who grieves the loss of his spouse, child, or friend may also be grieving an earlier loss. Death will bring up all those suppressed feelings of the past, compounding the emotional reactions of the present. Those who are suffering from old losses as well as recent ones will either have a double grief to suppress or a larger grief to release. Unless the latter occurs, the process will only continue to erode the survivor's well being — emotionally, physically, or mentally.

Supporting and Assisting the Young Survivor

A caregiver can provide support and assistance to the boy or adolescent in a number of ways.

- By providing an honest and meaningful explanation of the death

- By providing physical comfort and affection

- By encouraging but not forcing personal conversation and emotional expression

- By allowing the survivor to participate in funeral or memorial services (unless he prefers to be excluded)

- By keeping environmental changes to a minimum

- By allowing the survivor to participate in age-appropriate activities

- By making it possible for the survivor to experience ongoing support from an adult male

Providing an honest and meaningful explanation of the death. Immediately after the death, the surviving parent or closest caregiver is enduring multiple stresses. These are produced by the caregiver's own grief, the necessity to tell the child immediately, the caregiver's lack of physical energy or fear of "breakdown," and the conflict that often results from the need to tell and the desire to protect. So telling the young survivor of a death during the time of such severe family crisis is a most demanding and painful task. However, the message does need to be delivered to him, and the discussion conducted, as soon after the death as possible. Time is a crucial factor.

As the explanation is given, the adult should make every effort to:

1. Use language that is appropriate to the age of the child.

2. Use language that is free of philosophical, religious, or sentimental references.

3. Tell the truth about the death without giving unnecessary or disturbing details. This means telling the actual cause (He had a heart attack), the circumstances (He stopped breathing in the middle of the night and was taken to the hospital), and the chronology of what happened (The doctors tried very hard to save his life, but it wasn't possible. He died in the hospital. Now he has been taken to the funeral home.).

4. Understand that the child may not react in a way which is acceptable to adults. For example, due to his age, he may not respond with immediate sadness or sympathy. In fact, he may pretend not to hear what he is being told, or he may laugh.

Providing physical comfort and affection. Considering the many pressures on the parent or parents immediately after the death, it is not surprising that so many boys experience an absence of comfort after a death. But it cannot be emphasized enough that when boys are told of the loss of a loved one, there is too often a total lack of physical contact or affection. Instead, a statement about the death is made to the boy. The boy listens. As a result, the boy feels diminished by the loss, smaller in the world, and vulnerable. Throughout this period of shock and disorientation, it is very important for an emotional and physical connection to be made by someone who is respected and loved by the boy. A hug or kiss can bring a grieving child out of the cloud of fear and abandonment and into the circle of concern and understanding.

Throughout their childhood, it is a fact that boys are held less frequently than girls and for shorter periods of time. They are touched, caressed, and cuddled less often. Anyone knows that to be held by a trusted loved one is to be comforted. Even a mere pat on the arm or shoulder can break the invisible capsule of isolation in which a young survivor may find himself.

Encouraging but not forcing personal conversation and emotional expression. When a young survivor withdraws and appears to be bearing a loss alone, others may assume that he is coping with everything, dealing effectively with the loss, and making progress through the time of emotional pain, disorder, and transition. This may or may not be true; most likely, it is not.

When asked by the interviewer how he could have been helped when he was a young survivor, a retired businessman replied as follows:

Businessman: It might have been a good idea for the parent to share, to let the kid know how weak they feel, how vulnerable they feel,

	but they're going to make it, going to be all right, going to get through this.
Interviewer:	Did you ever have that kind of conversation with your parent?
Businessman:	Nothing like that. Ever.
Interviewer:	Did you ever talk about the loss to each other?
Businessman:	No. Never.

The young survivor should be encouraged to talk, to express his feelings, and to ask questions. The child's questions should be answered readily and honestly. If the child asks a question for which there seems to be no answer, then he should be told that the answer is unclear or unavailable, and as soon as there is more information it will be shared with him. It is important for the caregiver to listen to what the survivor is saying, and to express his or her own feelings and perhaps mention some fond memories of the dead loved one. When these are shared between a father and son or a mother and son, the exchange proves that the feelings are not bad nor unnecessary and that they will not destroy the survivors.

If a child asks questions or openly states feelings, the task of relieving them is made considerably easier. As one mother said, "When Daren started asking questions, I knew part of the battle had been won. I knew what was bothering him the most." A child feels a tremendous need to understand a death and to figure out his position within what now appears to be a frightening, insecure world.

These needs are not exclusively those of young children. They effect teenagers as well, though the inquiries come in different forms because they reflect a more mature level of development. The very young child will ask questions about where a dead person is, how he gets by, and when he will return. An older child who has a more highly developed concept of death will ask questions that cover a more abstract spectrum, such as "Did dad know it when he died?" "Why do good people have to suffer?" "What kind of God takes your mother away?"

I had strong feelings that there was no God. In other words, why me? Why my situation? There are so many bad people in the world, why did God kill these good people? We haven't done anything wrong. We're a perfectly nice family. My sister is a nice little girl, and I'm a nice little boy. My dad is a nice guy and everybody likes him. There's no God — or he's crazy.

(Adult survivor reflecting on the deaths of both his parents when they were in their thirties)

If a young survivor does not ask questions, the caregiving adult's task of "reading" the child is made more difficult. Often, however, a child who does not formulate his or her concerns into questions will indicate them through casual remarks or incidental actions. The caregiving adult can often facilitiate expression by putting the child's feelings into words. This technique is illustrated in these examples drawn from my earlier book, *Beyond Grief.*

Brent: I'm not going to play Little League. Jimmy's dad is the coach this year and Jimmy is always hanging around him.
Mother: I know you're probably wishing your dad were here like Jimmy's dad. I miss your dad very much, too. But you might like to try Little League for a while. Your brother and I will enjoy coming to your games this summer.

***

Jay: I never used to take out the garbage when Mom asked me to. I used to let it pile up until she got mad at me. I don't know why I was so mean.
Dad: I remember when you did that. Mom did get mad, but she understood that kids don't always do what you want them to when you want them to. She always knew how you felt about her and she certainly knew you weren't mean.

Openness, attentive listening, and observing are all vitally important. There should be equal receptivity to the negative feelings which the survivor may have, such as the anger, bitterness, guilt, jealousy, or resentment as well as to feelings of yearning, despair, or loneliness. Acceptance, honesty, and consistency provide solid stepping stones through anyone's grieving process.

Allowing the survivor to participate in funeral or memorial services (unless he prefers to be excluded). Being sent to his room, out to play, or to a friend's house immediately after the death of a parent or sibling, is a tale often told by the young survivor. It is essential during the time of the funeral preparation and service that the boy not be isolated and excluded. He knows a loved one has died. He will be better off listening and seeing than being shut away to sort out other family members' actions and feelings. The grieving boy does not "go outside and play," even if he appears to have done so. Regardless of what he seems to be doing, it will be the rare survivor who will not be feeling afraid, alone, isolated, confused, or ignored.

When a young survivor chooses to go to the funeral, an adult should then talk with him beforehand about what to expect. Depending upon the survivor's age and maturity, he will need to be informed about details like these:

- Where the funeral will be held

- What kind of room the family will be seated in

- Who will sit next to the child

- What the child will hear (music, a talk that will be about the loved one, prayers)

- Where the person who has died will be (in a closed casket, open casket, in another location)

- What other people may do (sit quietly, cry, come up to the child and hug him or talk to him)

- What the child should do when people express their condolences

- The reason for going to the cemetery and how the cemetery will look

When events, sights, and expectations for the boy's or adolescent's behavior are explained, the young survivor will be less anxious and frightened about the services. An informed youngster is better able to participate in the necessary customs and ceremonies when he feels aware, and at least somewhat confident.

If the young survivor enters into the activities that are taking place around him, he is joining others in dealing with the loss, rather than being put in the position of trying to pretend it didn't happen. Death is a family event, not an exclusively adult event.

Keeping environmental changes to a minimum. Death creates an enormous, painful void. When other losses are added to the loss of a loved one, the void gets even bigger and more painful. A boy or adolescent may be required to move from his bedroom, his school, or even his home town. Such an experience may be terrifying; yet he will, more than likely, suffer in silence.

> I had been popular in the town where we lived. That was all I knew. I had a lot of friends. I was popular and all that stuff. I didn't know anybody when we moved and, boy, I'll tell you I was afraid. I longed for friendship. I always felt like kind of a loner, so I wanted to have friends. It was through music that I made my first friend. Thank God I was in the band and orchestra.
>
> *(55-year-old survivor who was orphaned during 7th grade)*

Obviously, family circumstances sometimes make changes unavoidable. Pets may be given away or put to sleep. The family furniture or automobile may be sold. The young survivor's personal possessions may be pared down to accomodate moving, or to create additional space for another person who is joining the household.

Whenever possible, it is helpful for the changes in the young survivor's life to be counterbalanced by some well-established consistency in family habits and routines. Any survivor feels comfort in knowing there will be predictability to some events. A time frame can be established by the surviving parent or other caregiver which makes it possible for the child to anticipate events and to know there will be consistency in daily life. The boy will benefit from knowing that he can go to baseball practice at the park after school on Thursday and again on Saturday. Or that every Monday after dinner, he and his sister can go out for ice cream. Or that when he finishes his chores he can select something he would like to do during the week-end. A young child will be comforted by the fact that every Sunday night he can telephone Aunt Janice or Grandad for a few minutes. Consistency can be maintained, also, by setting specific meal times and bed times. Such routines give a sense of order to a world which has been disordered by death.

Allowing the survivor to participate in normal age-ap-propriate activites. When death occurs, roles of family members may shift, and a grieving boy may need to assume more respon-siblities than he had prior to the death.

> I had to do more work around the house, all that kind of stuff that my dad would normally do. I also became my own father in some ways. I had a tough childhood because I wasn't really allowed to be a kid too much after I was 16. I had to assume a lot of different roles. Then when I was in Vietnam, I had to assume the role of a healer. I always had to assume these roles and I never go to be a frivolous, young, happy teenager. I think now that's why I stay in tune with surfing. It's play. And I surf with a lot of my friends' kids and things.
>
> *(40-year-old reflecting on the loss of his father when the survivor was 16)*

It is crucial for the boy or adolescent not to be thrust into the role of the husband, father, or older brother who has died. A child in such a position, trying to take on the load of an older, more mature family member will ultimately be faced with some residual anger, bitterness, or regret for a lost childhood.

In an extreme case of delayed grief, a 72-year-old business executive recalled his reaction to the loss of his father when the boy was still an infant. He told of forfeiting his own childhood, becoming instead his mother's helper and protector. This be-havior continued from infancy into college. Finally, the man went through a ritual of letting his mother go so that he could continue his life without feeling compelled to play the part of his deceased father.   –

> In the early years, when I was around six or seven, I would hear my mother telling her neighbor friend about the death of her husband and she would start crying and I felt very bad. She didn't know I was overhearing at all. That situation set me up to playing the strong role later. I looked upon her as very weak, but close to her death I realized she was very, very

strong, even though outwardly she seemed meek and mild and weak.

The man went on to explain how his sense of responsiblity toward his mother influenced his behavior when he was a young man in college.

Whenever I got close in a relationship and I was serious enough to want to go steady with a girl, I would find a reason to break away. Then I met Louise my senior year in college, and I allowed myself to fall in love. Until all of a sudden you might say that my old self came back. The guy in the back said, "Hey, you're not free to have any serious relationship with any woman because you already have a wife. It's your mother. You have to be a responsible family person." Whenever I started to get serious with anyone, this inner feeling would come up: "Hey, you can't do that." So I started finding reasons to break off again. You might say this unconscious role was really running my life. What was most frustrating is I didn't know what was going on.

And when I broke up with the girl I cared about the most, I went through these feelings of "Am I going nuts?" I started having feelings of low self-confidence and at one point wanting to kill myself. Consciously, I knew I wouldn't do it, and didn't want to think in that direction, but the feeling welled up that the best thing to do is kill yourself. It scared me. The irony of it all is that the neurotic role I had with my mother kept me from killing myself. I knew if I killed myself it would kill her because I was her favorite son. But things were so bad I can easily sympathize with people who kill themselves.

It is important to note that a boy who helps out with his siblings and housework will learn patience, compassion, and how to assume domestic responsibilities. These are extremely valuable qualities and skills, but he must also be allowed time to develop his private interests, to nurture friendships with boys and girls his own age, and to feel confident about being an acceptable member of his peer group.

Making it possible for ongoing support to be available from an adult male. When a boy is enduring a loss, the support he receives will come more often from the female members of the family and community. While this attention is both nourishing and valuable, the young survivor can also benefit greatly from the attention and support of a father, an older brother, uncle, grandfather, or adult friend. Too often, a boy who loses a parent or sibling does without such support. In an interview with Dick, whose father died when Dick was 12 years old, he emphasized his need for male attention and commitment.

> *Interviewer:* What would you have wanted a male to do in order to make it easier for you?
>
> *Dick:* Answer questions. To be there for fairly mundane sorts of things. Availability. To have someone who is not someone who helps only in a major jam. But someone who should be available for simple things — to fix my bike, to talk about girls, to repair the lawnmower, day-to-day things. About a girl at school who I think likes me, a guy who says he'll beat me up.
>
> *Interviewer:* You didn't take those things to your mother...
>
> *Dick:* I couldn't. It was out of the question.
>
> *Interviewer:* Why?
>
> *Dick:* She was preoccupied with her own struggles. She was a woman. We were at odds. Not long after my father's death, that thing just grew and grew and there was a distance between us. We were strangers to each other. We were strangers in that house. There were a lot of things I had been conditioned to believe that you talk to dad about, not to mom. In the absence of dad, that means the questions don't get asked, not that now you ask them of her.

Interviewer:	Did you talk to her about your feelings at all?
Dick:	If at all, very little. I didn't discuss my feelings with her.

This same theme is reinforced by David whose sister died when he was 16 years old and whose father died when David was 18.

Interviewer:	At that period of time what would you have appreciated most from another human being?
David:	An older person to take me under their wing, like an older brother or someone like that.
Interviewer:	And talk to you about things that were...emotional?
David:	Yes! Show an interest in me. I never felt that anybody really cared for me, or was concerned about me.
Interviewer:	Your mother?
David:	Well, she was concerned but she was so wrapped up in herself.
Interviewer:	In her own grief?
David:	In her own grief, in wanting things better for herself. She wasn't really in much of a position to give.

It is common for the surviving teenager to perceive emotional discussions with his mother to be off limits. It is certainly true that a woman who loses her husband has plenty of emotional, mental, and physical demands and needs of her own to cope with; and, at the same time, she is trying to maintain a household, and figure out a plan of action which will prove workable for the remaining family members. A woman cannot be expected, regardless of how capable, caring, and determined she is, to meet all of the emotional needs of each surviving child. A mother may be superhuman in her abilities and energies, but the fact is, the boy or adolescent survivor will still benefit in a different way from the validation and attention from an older, trusted man.

There are many ways such an adult can help fill the youngster's painful void. Depending on the survivor's age, the relative or friend may read to him or tell him stories, repair his toys, praise his school work, discuss the young survivor's worries and fears with him, encourage his special interests, share sports events or other interests, or help him to decide on a college or a career choice. Any child or adolescent can benefit from such adult attention, but the young survivor may be saved from experiencing great emotional difficulty later by having such concern included in his life at a most crucial, needy time.

It's important to stress that a male relative or friend who makes false promises to a boy or adolescent does more harm than one who does not suggest any further contact. *Making a commitment to a grieving child is very serious business.*

> A vivid memory I have, that irritates me to this day, is of when my uncles gathered after my father's death, and they had come to eat and sit on the sofa and puff their cigars. And then there I am. I'm still just a zombie. My father had only been dead a few days. The funeral was just over. And it's all just a blur. Oh, they were all going to virtually adopt me. All the things they were going to do with me! They'd see to it that I'd get this and I'd get that and they'd take me hunting and they'd take me fishing and they'd get me in the Boy Scouts and they'd get me in De Molay and they were going to be a big part of my life and were going to take dad's place. And when they went out the door, I didn't see those men again for years and years.
>
> *(35-year-old reflecting on his father's death when the survivor was in the 8th grade.)*

Tony, an orphaned survivor, was sent from one foster home to another from the time he was five years old. He never had any reliable, consistent, and loving person in his life. By the time he was 15 years old, he never expected to have. He had given up. "Every time I ever called somebody Mama, then I had to move," he said. With his hopes dashed for any consistent, dependable love, certainly for any family, Tony now expresses the wish to end up in a town he likes when he is 18 and no longer at the mercy of the court.

For many young male survivors, hope of any kind is hard to come by. The promise of enjoying life without feeling isolated or full of despair is small. For that reason, every helpful act that can be performed by those close to him should be. "We are different," one teenaged survivor told another. "But there's a benefit in that. We've already been through hell. It isn't something ahead of us. It's in our past."

But, with grief, the past is only past when it has been dealt with; otherwise it pervades the present and threatens the future. When grief is addressed, when the painful emotions that accompany the loss of a loved one are expressed, when encouragement and emotional support are there for the grieving boy or adolescent, then he will be able to assign his early grief to those days of the past, rather than to the days in his life that are yet to be experienced.

5

Experiencing the Loss of a Parent as an Adult Survivor

Many times since the funeral when certain things have gone wrong, when I'm under some sort of trauma or stress, I would like to talk to him about something that's happening with my own kids, or my wife, or my life in general, I wish I had somebody like him to talk to. Sometimes I remember him and I cry....

...I planted a tree on his behalf. I had mom come up and we did a little ceremony for my father. I got his old pair of shoes and put them in the ground with the tree. He was a lumberman so I tried to do hardwood...It's taken me years....

(42-YEAR-OLD SURVIVOR)

Currently, the life expectancy of men is approximately 71.5 years, and that of women is 78.3 years. This means that a man is very likely to first experience the death of a loved one when his mother or father dies, and usually when this death occurs the grown son is in his forties or fifties.

One might think that since a parent is expected to pre-decease a son, the son would be minimally affected. Research has shown that this is not the case. Whether or not his parent's death was anticipated does not significantly affect the son's response to the death. (Also, unmarried men tend to suffer the loss of a parent even more than those who are married.)

Responding to Your Parent's Death

If you're surviving the loss of your mother or father, you may find yourself experiencing one or more of the following responses:

- Feeling abandoned
- Feeling closer to death
- Feeling vulnerable
- Feeling frustrated
- Feeling relieved and released

Feeling Abandoned

Many men confide that they never really expected their mother or father to die. They knew, logically, that parents do die, but not their parent, and not now.

> My sort of naive feeling was, well, things just sort of go on in this nice pleasant way. Here's my nice little mom and dad and their nice little house and everything will always be wonderful, on into eternity.
> (43-year-old survivor of parental death)

If you had always felt that a parental death was something that only happens to someone else, or would not happen to you until much later, you may suddenly feel abandoned and forsaken. You may find yourself having moments that, as one man described them, "are like an electric shock to the consciousness, a startling void." Such a state of disorientation can produce a wide variety of feelings, among which the most common are anger, sadness, anxiety, and fear.

A man who has suffered the loss of both his parents will sometimes say, "Now I feel like an orphan." Depending on the type of relationship you had with your parents, their deaths may make you feel orphaned and it may take away your home — either emotionally, physically, or both. You may have considered your parent's home as a sanctuary, a place of retreat, nurturance, or challenge. Or it may even have produced in you a feeling of extreme emotional discomfort. Whatever its significance, your parent's home is irretrievably removed from you when your second parent dies. One survivor summed up his feelings by saying, "Now I have no home to go to and no home to run away from."

Feeling Closer to Death

Until your parent dies, you are one generation away from your own death. When your second parent dies, you then become acutely aware that you are the next in succession to die. You may respond to this reality in an endless number of ways. You may reassess your future, speculate regarding the number of years you think you have left, and examine how your plans and goals fit into the remaining span of your life. As a result, you may make some readjustments. Your areas of interest may change. You may be more intent on increasing your income, or reducing it. You could become more health conscious, or focus more attention on your children or on strengthening your marital relationship. You may think more deeply and intently about the legacy you will leave.

But survivors sometimes take less constructive actions. For example, a man may do everything he can to deny that he is now the senior figure, that he has moved a notch closer to death. This latter factor may cause him to spend more, drink more, take more chances, or get involved in more absorbing yet less effective tasks. In such a mode, he blurs his own mortality and, at the extreme, ultimately hastens his own death. Suicide attempts appear to increase among this survivor group.

Feeling Vulnerable

If you ever experienced the loss of a job, car, position, plan, dream, or friendship, you endured the removal of something that you treasured as a special part of your immediate life — or even as an extension of yourself.

A loss of any sort makes a person feel vulnerable and lacking in the confidence or capability he would normally have. The death of your parent may now produce in you the ultimate in vulnerability because you had no control over the event which took your father or mother away. Nothing you could do, say, buy, think, bargain for, or threaten was able to prolong your parent's life.

Feeling Frustrated

The death of your parent may also leave you with some (or many) of your sentiments unexpressed. Because of this, your parents' death becomes the catalyst for the resolution of unfinished business. Such "business" can produce frustrations, and in cases where thoughts about it become obsessive, may cause you to suffer extreme personal torment.

Before dying, your parent may have confided some new bit of information to you which opened up emotional wounds, gave new insights, offered challenges, or committed you to carrying out an especially difficult final request. It's possible for such a confidence to cause you to feel emotionally impotent or inept, or you may feel that you are betraying some kind of trust which has been designated to you. Or you may even feel that if you had been allowed more time, or a slightly different set of circumstances, you could have saved your mother or father from death. Any number of frustrating circumstances can arise as a result of your suddenly being forced to bridge the distance between yourself and your parent when you learned that your parent's death was clearly eminent.

Feeling Relieved and Released

Some survivors view their parent's death as a relief, or a release from "being trapped." During the final months or years of their parent's life, they experienced a role reversal in which the son became the parent to his father or mother. This is particularly likely to have happened if the parent was terminally ill or the victim of senility.

Such a survivor may have attended to his parent's physical and emotional needs and met many demands which were similar to those which would be made by a child. Even though the son didn't want to assume the parenting role, he was forced to do so in order to maintain the parent's safety and to administer or monitor his or her health care. As a result, the son has memories which cause him undue emotional distress after the death.

> He said, "Don't put me in the hospital. Don't do it." I was on his couch and I could hear him in his room, groaning and moaning and in pain. He said, "I want to die at home." Finally, about two or three in the morning, I did call the hospital. He couldn't walk and the ulcer was very, very painful, so I had to make that decision. You go against his wishes to call the ambulance but you have to make that choice.
>
> *(32-year-old man reflecting on his father's final days)*

At the same time, the son may have a sense of relief after the death because his compulsive caretaking is no longer necessary. He finds himself suddenly freed from a very consuming responsibility and is able to focus on other people or responsibilities which have long been neglected.

Relief and release can be experienced by a survivor for a number of other reasons, as well. In some cases a son may have had such lifelong difficulty in his relationship with his parent that he is pleased not to have to cope with the tension or dissention any longer.

> I experienced relief that my father died. I was very aware of being glad that he was out of my life. I was also sad that he died, but I had a combination of feelings. I viewed his inability to communicate and to understand as the root of the problem we had.
>
> *(Survivor of sibling and parental death)*

Not surprisingly, such feelings of relief and release are often accompanied by guilt.

The Special Issues of Surviving a Mother's Death

> When the world of men is submerged in the world of technology and business, it seems to the boy that cool excitement lies there, and warm excitement with the mother; money with the father, food with the mother; anxiety with the father, assurance with the mother; conditional love with the father, and unconditional love with the mother....
>
> ...the boy...learns cultural feeling, verbal feeling, discrimination of feeling almost entirely from his mother. Bonding requires physical closeness, a sense of protection, approval of one's very being, conversation in which feelings and longings can step out, and some attention which the young male can feel as *care for the soul*. The boy in the United States receives almost all of these qualities, if he receives them at all, from the mother, and so his bonding takes place with her, not with the father....There are many exceptions to this generalization, of course, but most of the exceptions I met were in men who worked in some physical ways with their fathers as carpenters, woodcutters, musicians, farmers, etc.
>
> (Robert Bly, "Men's Initiation Rites," *Utne Reader*)

When you lose your mother, you usually lose the person who shaped your early years, who taught you how to walk, talk, behave — how to *be* in the world. Aside from fulfilling a number of other important roles, your mother may have been your strongest guide, your severest critic, or your only refuge for many, many years.

Very often, as compared to your father, your mother was the major communicator, the translator, or confidante. When she died, you may have been left without an intermediary, a buffer, or a referee. If so, you may now have difficulty interacting with a father who makes meaningful conversation a laborious process, if not an impossible one. Your father's silent message may be that "talking is for women." This aversion to communication is illustrated in many households by the way telephone calls are handled. Robert Bly points out, "So many American fathers, if they answer the phone when a son or daughter calls, will usually say after a moment, 'Here's your mother.' "

Whatever the specific role or roles your mother played during your life, they're removed forever when she dies. Regardless of what your own role was — independent son, dependent son, "husband substitute," or friend — that role is also eliminated from your life. As a result, you are faced with a period of reorganization and transition.

The relationship you had with your mother will have even more dimensions if your father died during your youth, leaving your mother to raise you on her own. As pointed out in chapter 4, the boy or adolescent who loses his father may relate to his mother in a number of ways. He may protect her from his own feelings of grief, his yearnings for a father, his fears, or his feelings of emptiness and resentment.

> I had resentment toward my mother which was
> expressed in very subtle ways. Even though I was
> good to my mother, and people praised me for being
> good to my mother, inside me there were times I
> resented having to do things and I felt bad about it.
> Any advice or remark from my mother, I looked on as
> nagging. I was sort of in this multi-relationship of
> being a son, father, and husband all at the same time.
> There were times that even though I was driving her
> to see her friends, I was resenting that I had to
> provide time to her, so I would drive fast, almost
> scaring her. And then I felt guilty about it.
>
> *(72-year-old man reflecting on his
> father's death during the survivor's
> .infancy)*

Any man whose father died and whose mother did not remarry may feel very responsible for how her life turned out, for her aloneness (either perceived or actual), and her devotion to her children at the expense of her own personal life.

> We kind of knew that it was for our sake that she
> didn't remarry. There were men who proposed to her,
> but she told us, "I've heard that stepchildren are very
> poorly treated, and I don't want to take the chance

that you three would be badly treated if I were to remarry."

(*Survivor of father's death during son's infancy*)

The mother who makes a conscious choice not to remarry because she prefers being single may still find it hard to convince her sons of her preference. Even if she feels complete and satisfied with her choice, her son may see his mother as having led an unrequited life, and may carry that guilt and responsibility on into his adult years.

The extent to which a mother's death affects her son may not be at all evident. The son's adult life may be shaped by the loss without recognition of the fact by himself or others. As mentioned in chapter 2, one such example is found in the life of the famous Houdini.

Karl Menninger points out in *Man Against Himself* that Houdini's "most dramatic escapes were from coffins buried underground and from chains while underwater. Coupled with this, unconsciously, is the fact that he had an extraordinary attachment for his mother which strongly affected his entire life." On the anniversary of his mother's death in 1925 he inserted in his diary a copy of Masefield's poem to his mother:

"In the dark womb where I began
My mother's life made me a man.
Through all the months of human birth
Her beauty fed my common earth.
I cannot see, nor breathe, nor stir,
But through the death of some of her."

(*The Poems and Plays of John Masefield*)

In his diary, Houdini wrote, "Many a bitter tear I am shedding....Had terrible spell after show on account of my darling Mother." A mother's death can indeed have a profound effect on the life of a man. After your mother has died you may have a powerfully strong need to create a connection you can see, something you can hold in your hand as a symbol of your love for her, as proof of your special relationship. A male survivor told the following story of how he managed to keep tangible evidence of the love he and his mother shared.

> When I was a little kid I had bought her a pin, and it was something she kept forever and ever and always would wear. She liked it. When she died, what I did was I took the pin before the funeral and I cut the pin in half. In the Jewish religion, the coffin is supposed to be shut, but I went in the funeral home, opened the coffin and pinned it on her, and I kept the other half. Now I will never forget the incident when that was the last time I saw her. It's a symbol of never parting.... When I first went to the funeral home and the coffin was there I met my aunt and couple of other cousins. I opened it up and I wanted to see her. But everybody was around. But the next day, the day of the funeral, when I came back and did this, only one other person was around and it was more like a secret that we had, more of a shared experience, a symbol of love.
>
> *(40-year-old survivor of parental and sibling death)*

A man whose mother was a sculptor swore to "turn nothings into somethings, as she did." He recalled when he was a child she would hand him a lump of clay to amuse himself with as she worked; after her death, he sought to identify with her art. "It was hard to be the son of an artist," he recalled, but at the same time he vowed to continue her work, to honor her through his own creativity.

The Special Issues of Surviving a Father's Death

Following the death of their fathers, sons often express the need to find out more about the men who were their fathers, particularly about the emotional aspects of their father's lives. Because many fathers are emotionally unavailable for the greater portion of their son's lives, the sons may have very little knowledge, if any, of their father's emotional needs, drives, and rewards.

The thing that bothered me most about my father was
that I could never get his attention. It turned out that
none of the others could either.

*(Survivor of parental loss, one of
four siblings)*

Most fathers are unknown to their children because
they are physically absent much of the time and often
absent-minded toward their children when they are at
home. Even there, they are otherwise engaged, fixing
the car, raking leaves, watching televison, jogging, or
paying bills. The resentment that fathers so often
project when they are at home is often a sign of
denied and hidden envy or jealousy, of the wish to be
emotionally absent.

A child must learn to deal with both the real and
the emotional absences of a father — the father's anger,
envy or emotional distance — and the child's own
imagery about that absence or distance. For most men
struggle not with their actual fathers, but with their
internalized images: the absent father does not care; the
angry father is an ogre.

The father who dies can never be perceived as a
benevolent figure if the child cuts him off when he
dies, resenting the death and concluding, "I never had
a father," as a way of numbing the pain of loss. The
father who "never was" becomes the absent father, the
chilling father who does not care. He is the product of
a child's ingratitude and resentment. But the dead
father gave his child the gift of life and many other
genetic, psychological, and perhaps material gifts and
guidance. A son's reconnecting to his dead father, even
late in life, can cause profound psychological healing.

(Stephen Shapiro, *Manhood*)

Exploring and Defining the Father

As sons reflect on the death of their fathers, they express the
desire to find out certain things about them. These can be summed up, most aptly, by the question, "Who were you?"

I would ask him, knowing what he does now, how he
would change his life in any way. If he could have
changed anything in his life, what would it have been?
A lot of times I wasn't really certain where he stood
on some things. That would have answered my
curiosity.

> (40-year-old survivor of father's
> death)

A man whose father died after the boy's parents were
divorced answered this way when asked, "If you could talk to
your father now, and just say one sentence to him, what would
it be?"

It would be a question. Rather than telling something,
I would want to ask him things about his life. Who are
you? I would want to know more of the things I never
got a chance to learn. I don't know that much about
him, and yet I feel him. So I would want to ask who
he is so I could choose some of it for myself.

> (43-year-old reflecting on his
> father's death during the survivor's
> early manhood)

If you find yourself reviewing who and what your father
was, you may have a desire to determine for yourself exactly
what your father stood for. You may feel as if you want to gain
a fuller understanding of the qualities that need and deserve to
be perpetuated or the characteristics which are less than positive.
In the statements which follow, this avenue of exploration is reflected by four individual survivors.

When I passed 43 I said, "I just outlived my father."
When I had my 44th birthday, then I said, "Well now, I
know I've outlived my father." I felt a bit of trepidation
and a bit of anticipation, like uncharted territory. I
lived through some times when I could have gone the
way of my father, chosen my weakness instead of my
strength. With both my mother and my father, there
were things I could use and things that would take me
to a place I didn't want to go. It's a question of

choosing the strengths and not the weaknesses, and trying not to confuse one for the other.

***

He had a dignity, which probably verged on being overly proud. But I think it was a beautiful trait and I think he was a highly disciplined man. That's a trait that I have and I admire. I didn't really see those as positive attributes as I was growing up.

***

My father was a really good person and he tried his best, but he had an impossible task which was to live up to his father's expectations. And my father, because those expectations were impossible, always failed, and was regretting. As amazingly capable as my father was, it was like his life was cursed. He had a tough row to hoe. He was gone a lot and working a lot.

***

He always liked a good joke. I am the same way. He had a certain moral code. Hard working. I'm very hard working, and very independent.

***

A man formulates certain images of his father and holds in high regard specific traits or characteristics which he admires and would like to claim as his own. "Hard working," "independent," "dignified," "proud," and "moral" are words often used by sons to characterize their fathers positively. Coupled with these positive attributes are often descriptions of fathers being "distant," "remote," "silent," or "impersonal."

It isn't surprising that when fathers die, the objects and mementoes most often treasured by their sons seem to be those things that were work-related or related to nature, rather than those possessions to which an emotional attachment would more obviously be attributed.

One of the things I have of my father's is an old chalk box, a carpenter's chalk box with a string on it, because he was a general contractor and I heard about the good work he did, and all that, so it was kind of neat to have that box.

(40-year-old whose father died during the survivor's teenage years)

As you reflect on your father's life, you may see him as having to overcome tremendous obstacles, hardship, and unrealistic demands. You may even see your father as a victim, doomed in some respects because of the demands placed on him, the "bad luck" he had, the loads he had to bear, the silence with which he bore it. "My old man," a surviving son will say, "he worked his ass off." But, as has been pointed out, the absorption in work — whether of necessity or desire — often resulted in the father being emotionally remote and unavailable to his son.

There is another dimension to father loss that some survivors have experienced; it is feeling released from their father's control. Such a survivor may have suffered as a result of his father exerting control over the son's life through the use of money, power, or position, or the son may have felt his father's control in less direct ways, through manipulation, expectation, "guidance," or favoritism toward a "good" sibling or "successful" brother or sister. The messages he gave his son may have been overt, such as spoken approval or disapproval, or they may have been more subtly conveyed, taking the form of implied disappointment.

It's almost like being in the shadow of a father was really an overwhelming thing. Still, years later after the death, still I'm feeling the shadow. There wasn't much praise from him. It was usually things that were being done wrong...or things that I needed to do.

(35-year-old survivor)

I felt much less accountable after my father died. And much freer because he was very controlling. That difficult area of my life was gone. So that is where the relief comes from....

(40-year-old whose father died when the survivor was 18)

Sometimes a man can grow into a man only when his father dies; sometimes it is a father's absence or illness

that releases the son's potential to mature. The
expectation that father must always be there as a
protector is the shield of boyhood, but it is the enemy
of manhood.

(Stephen Shapiro, *Manhood*)

Identifying With the Dead Father

A woman whose father died when she and her brother were
in their thirties told the story of her brother's sudden transformation following their father's death:

My father came from Tennessee. He was the kind of
man who wore overalls, worked on his farm, chopped
wood, and always had the kids working alongside, if
they wanted to. All of a sudden after our dad died,
my brother, who had spent most of his life in Northern
California, started talking with a Tennessee accent. He
moved out in the country. He had his own little farm.
When my son and I went to visit him, I couldn't
believe my eyes. There he was in overalls, walking just
like my father did — in a kind of lope — and saying
things like, "Wanna help me, boy? Bring me the saw
then, boy, and come on." My *brother* had become my
father.

An identification with another person can be manifested
mentally, emotionally, socially, physically, or materially. Often the
survivor becomes acutely aware of identification with a mother
or father during the mental review process that takes place after
the parent's death. The silent questions are asked: *Are* we alike?
In what way are we alike?

Some survivors make a conscious selection of the qualities,
traits, skills, interests, mannerisms, eccentricities, or goals to be
perpetuated. Other survivors have a subconscious identification
process; with still others, it is completely absent.

For example, identification may mean that the survivor uses
a figure of speech that was unique to the parent, emulates a gesture, has the same habit or seeks out the same kinds of friends
the parent had. He or she may dress similarly, carry out a parent's
dream or wish, participate in an organization or work for a cause

in which the parent was interested. This type of identification, which is not harmful, may offer a great deal of satisfaction.

If, however, the grieving person feels the compulsion to follow in the parent's footsteps or to emulate the parent's behavior, when he does not genuinely want to do so, or does not have the required skills or abilities, the identification process will not facilitate grieving, but distort it.

Incorporating the Essence

There is a difference between *identifying with* the parent and *incorporating* the dead parent's essence. This is a concept that may not be readily understood by others because it is something a son feels and it cannot be easily described. Such a process begins with the realization that the survivor has *inside himself* the essence, the spirit, the valuable core of the parent who died. It is linked to carrying on and continuing.

After the death of your parent, you become your own parent. As you continue on, you're likely to retain and nourish within yourself some old "family familiar," life-enhancing properties which you believe have been passed on to you.

> The realization came...it finally hit me that he wasn't
> gone. There was a point where I realized that there
> was something about his essence entering into me and
> the fact that I was him, and that he had carried the
> baton as far as he could and he had handed it to
> me...and now it was my job to go further. And that
> realization was really helpful.
> (*35-year-old survivor of his father's
> death*)

This kind of "incorporation" of your parent makes necessary a selection process. You'll undoubtedly try to leave behind, as best as you can, the negative and painful elements of your parent's spirit. Then you can select and sustain within yourself everything you wish to keep, such as a certain morality, honor, or dignity. And you can progress through your life, gathering, enriching, and expanding what you already are by virtue of your unique heritage.

6

Experiencing Loss
as a Husband

*When I wake up, it's horrendous. I'm going from a
fairyland of relaxation, rest, and complete
composure to waking up into this bad real world
where my wife isn't here. It's so comforting, so
restful, so peaceful, and then you wake up, and it's
like jumping into a swimming pool with 15-degree
water. This reality, this, "Oh, my God, here we are
again, Dick. Your wife is dead and you're all
alone." I don't want to wake up. I'd just as soon
sleep forever.*

(WIDOWER WHO HAD BEEN
MARRIED 40 YEARS)

After the death of your wife you'll find yourself trying to contend
with a variety of painful emotions, conditions, and reactions. In
fact, it's quite possible that you'll be immersed in a world of feelings you never knew existed. You may feel very isolated and
alone in your grief, stunned by what has happened to your life,
and astounded at how it has suddenly, dramatically changed.

Some days the pendulum of emotion may seem to swing
back and forth, causing your feelings to alternate between quiet
desolation and inner chaos. Your response may be to express your
feelings of grief or to suppress them — to keep them "underground," thereby short-circuiting the normal grieving process.

Responding to Your Wife's Death

Every widower has some unique individual reactions to the loss of his wife, but generally you'll be likely to respond to your wife's death in one or more of the following ways:

- You may feel dismembered.

- You may recognize that the dimensions of your loss extend beyond your previous awareness of them (that is, that the scope and depth of your wife's roles were not fully recognized).

- You may undergo a painful self-examination.

- You may experience physiological or psychological symptoms.

Feeling Dismembered

When you lose your wife, you feel as if an essential part of yourself has been cut away or removed. You feel incomplete. When you talk about the death, either to yourself or others, you may find yourself using the words "cut" or "carved" to describe your wife's absence from your life. You may say "I feel as if part of me has been carved away," or "My wife's death was like cutting off part of me," or "Half of me is missing." Such descriptions and feelings make perfect sense because the death of your wife is equivalent to surgery — emotional surgery. When she died you were left to deal with an open wound and a heart that may indeed seem broken.

Recognizing the Full Scope and Dimension of the Loss

Along with feeling dismembered, you find that a great many facets of your life were completely dependent upon or very closely attached to your wife's presence. When your wife was living, you viewed her principally as your partner and as your children's mother. But after her death, the wide variety of roles your wife filled during your marriage become much more explicit and painfully real to you. You may now discover that area after area within your life is deeply affected because its central figure is missing.

She was my right arm, my co-pilot, my best friend, my buddy. She was everything. We went everywhere together. For example, if I were to go to the store, she would go with me. If she went down the road two blocks, I would go with her. We were always together. Occasionally, I would like to see her go out in her car by herself. If she were to be gone for an hour, I would be at the window in forty minutes, waiting to see her car coming down the road. Twenty minutes I would stand at this window. I couldn't wait until she came back. To see her coming down that hill and pull up in the driveway after an absence was almost orgasmic. That's how it was. She felt the same way about me.

(66-year-old widower)

When most men discuss the losses they feel after their wife's death, they stress the importance of her three main roles: domestic partner, sexual partner, and companion.

You lose your domestic partner. You don't really realize how much a woman does. She does all the housework. She makes the bed, tears it all apart piece by piece. There's a lot of work there. To dust, clean, and keep the house up. You miss that. So you miss your domestic partner and also you miss your companion to go out to dinner, and a companion for social events. You miss your sexual partner. Depending upon your age, that can be very, very important — very, very dramatic. I have a lot of friends that *that* [sex] would be second. They would miss the presence of their wife, but sex would be right up there at the top of the list.

(67-year-old widower)

Domestic Partner

Even though you may have shared in the cooking, or done the grocery shopping, or waxed the floor once in awhile, you now find yourself having to manage all of the domestic responsiblities. If you're not taking care of them yourself, you've had to find someone who will. In fact, you may discover that some necessary facets of your domestic maintenance have never before come to your attention. You may say, "I never realized how much she did," or "I don't know how she took care of all these things. She had her system, but I can't seem to get it all done." Cooking, shopping, washing clothes, cleaning the house, and buying clothing and household items may all need to be worked into your already overflowing schedule unless you are able to hire help, or you have a relative or friend who is assisting you with some of the tasks.

Of course, if you have children you'll also have to assume or oversee all the child-rearing tasks which you formerly shared with your wife, or only observed. In addition to being responsive and sensitive to your children's emotional needs, you must now see that your children's schedules are met, their clothes maintained, their homework attended to, and their appointments made and kept. You may find yourself feeling overwhelmed when such a diverse barrage of relatively unfamiliar responsibilities shout for attention all at once.

Sexual Partner

Along with missing your domestic partner, you'll have strong feelings about losing your sexual partner. Most likely, your loss may make you feel abandoned and frustrated or desolately lonely and frightened. Suddenly your physically intimate life, as you knew it, is gone. The intimacy that you and your wife shared may have been a consistent part of your life for only a few months, or for a decade or so, or it may even have spanned fifty years or more. You long for your wife's touch, smell, and voice. You may keep her clothes as reminders and talismans. It's your way of treasuring your loved one's scent, the uniqueness of her person, and her favorite colors and styles, and, at the same time, providing a sort of tactile comfort to yourself. It's reassuring and perfectly normal.

As you endure the loss of your familiar sexual partner, you may find yourself plagued by a number of very disturbing sexual fears. You may even be haunted by one or more of these questions:

- Does being without my wife mean that I'll be without sex for the rest of my life?

- What if I can't have sex? Does being a widower mean I'm going to be impotent?

- What if I don't know how to please any other woman?

- How long should I wait before I'm with another woman?

Some widowers fear they won't be able to find a willing sexual partner or to satisfy a new partner. Others report having an exceedingly strong sex drive that seems to dominate a lot of their thoughts and actions. Such conditions and fears can be pervasive for a considerable period of time after a man loses his wife.

Some widowers *decide* that they're impotent, as if that is the natural, inevitable outcome of losing a wife.

> I found out I'm impotent. The impotency thing will go away...it sure would be terrible if it didn't. A man, you know, his virility is the one thing that satisfies his ego. If that's all he did was lose his virility, then he'd probably think what the hell else is there to *live* for.
> *(61-year-old widower)*

While the fear of impotency is very real, the actuality of being impotent is not. Such a condition usually occurs quite suddenly, isn't permanent, and subsides as the man progresses through the grieving period. During this time, some men feel the need for emotional intensity, kissing, hugging, affection, and tenderness. But more often, widowed men will feel they cannot experience such intimacy unless it includes sexual intercourse.

Companion

Another great part of your grief arises from missing your wife as your companion. In fact, your wife may very well have been the only companion you had for many years, or since the beginning of your marriage.

In *The Hazards of Being Male*, Herb Goldberg reports that "The male unconsciously comes to see the female as his lifeline — his connection to survival and his energy source. Many adult men, once they have established a primary relationship with a woman, begin to abandon almost all of their other relationships."

> In our little town people always used to say, "Oh, we admire you so much. You're always riding your bikes together and walking down the street hand in hand."

Friends of mine commented, "As close as you are to your wife, and as close as she is to you, what in the hell would you do if something happened to the other?" I would say, "I'm not going to worry about that because she's going to outlive me. She's plenty healthy. She is a vegetarian, takes vitamins, takes a lot of precautions."

Another thing that really bothers me is to see people my age walking hand in hand or sitting in the candlelight having dinner. They don't realize how really lucky they are, sitting there by candlelight having dinner and enjoying themselves and being alive and healthy. You know, it's just such a simple thing to ask for. And then they walk by. It just really bothers me. I've never envied anybody in my life. I've always been glad I'm me. I've earned a good living and had the best wife in the world. There wasn't a reason to envy anybody. But now I envy people my age who have their spouses and who are healthy and they are together and holding hands. You don't know what it does to me when I see that. It does me in. I never thought I'd envy anybody.

(66-year-old widower)

If your wife filled the role of constant companion, you may have seen her as your defender as well; that is, she served as your foil when it was necessary, as your defense against the world. One widower reflected the sentiments of many survivors when he said, "She was the only one between me and the world, the only one I completely trusted. She was the person who made the world make sense." If you have similar feelings about your wife, her death will now require you to face the world with no intermediary, to get through the day without being able to talk to your best friend, and to continue on in your life even though your life's main focus is missing.

As you recognize the many and various capacities that your wife filled, you may find yourself reviewing the type of behavior you engaged in during your marriage. You may survey the way in which your own roles did or did not augment the roles your wife filled. You may see yourself as having complemented her roles, coincided with them, or been in opposition to them.

Undergoing Painful Self-Examination

As you survive the loss of your wife, you'll almost certainly feel some guilt or anger. You may feel guilty for not "loving enough," which means not showing how you felt, talking about it, giving cards or gifts, expressing your affection, or not recognizing the depth of your own love.

> When Marina died, I acutely knew what true love was — when it was no longer available to give or to receive. And the hollow of that experience has grown steadily and heavily as the initial shock that carved it out of me has wearily eroded.
> (C. L. Sulzberger, *How I Committed Suicide*)

You may torment yourself with numerous "flashbacks" into your life with your wife, scenes in which you did not do something that would have conveyed your love, eased your wife's load, or made her life physically easier or more emotionally satisfying.

> Not yet expurgated, says my aching heart to my calm head. Some of the scars are well healed, others paper thin; it is like walking through a recently burned forest, where one never knows if the ground will collapse into a creeping underground fire pit. As I plod through the monotony of domestic chores, I think of Barbara longing to break free to paint or spin or do theatre work, but saying nothing. As I am ill, alone, moaning and indulging myself, I remember how Barbara never could be ill when the kids were small; I didn't help enough. Yes, I forgive me my imperfections, but I really did not look, I really did not see that with a small sacrifice on my part she would have experienced a great gain in hers.
> (*From the letters of a 64-year-old widower*)

In addition to experiencing various forms of remorse, you may feel some strong surges of anger during your grieving process. The anger may be toward your wife for dying and leaving you by yourself to feel lonely, confused, or even physically ill. You may experience anger toward yourself for not foreseeing and preventing her death, for not getting a different doctor, medical treatment, hospital, or clinic. You may be angry for allowing yourself to become vulnerable to another person and needy, "in so deep," or "so attached."

As has been pointed out previously, anger is linked to a loss of power and control. Death, of course, takes away both power and control. Some of your surface feelings may be covering up your hidden and heartrending cry: "What am I supposed to do now?"

Your self-examination may reveal to you that you're not a loner, that you need other people around you, and that, in fact, loneliness is sometimes nearly more than you can bear.

> I don't like to be alone. I've always tried to find a
> buddy. When I was in the army and I was in a group,
> I always tried to find a buddy right away and I would
> look forward to us to go out on weekend passes and
> look for women — that's the favorite pastime of GI's —
> and try to find a date, but I wasn't going to do that by
> myself. I had to have a buddy. We'd go out and have
> a steak dinner and chase women. If I'd be flying, and
> my mealtime didn't coincide with his, I'd feel really
> bad. When I left, or he left, or we had to split up, I
> would have a kind of grief just like I'm having now
> until I found someone else. I'm just not a loner.
> *(Widower who was married
> 40 years)*

The loneliness you experience now takes on new meaning because it's a kind of loneliness you never experienced before, one you never thought you would have to endure.

> I haven't cleaned out her drawers. I haven't cleaned
> out her purse. I went through a real trauma when I
> had to get into her purse and get the car keys. Believe
> me, I was a basket case by the time I got the keys off
> the key ring. I cried for about two hours. I couldn't do
> anything. I was just immobile....
>   What I need is a pair of stockings hanging over
> the shower, a shower cap on the showerhead, cologne,

a woman's presence. I appreciate that — and it's
missing. I'm not a loner.

(65-year-old widower)

To experience loneliness is to examine the self, to become
acutely aware of it as a separate entity, away from the context of
any relationship. The self is viewed apart from the influences that
surround it, independent of whatever satellites normally move
around its orb. As Anthony Storr states in his excellent book, *Solitude*, "The capacity to be alone...becomes linked with self-discovery and self-realization, with becoming aware of one's deepest
needs, feelings and impulses." In this sense, the self becomes a
thing alone. It has no past or future. It is here and now and singular. Such self-examination is reflected in this widower's letter:

The music is over, and the quietness of the fall
afternoon comes creeping in, to my increasing
discomfort. How strange it is that I can't live within
my own head, which is so full of fertile ideas, and
information, and intuition. I wonder what genetic or
environmental circumstance made me so very complete
in so many ways, so utterly incomplete in others? I'm
ill at ease in the silence of my own familiar home. I've
a hundred friends I can ring and talk to, but that's no
good — the answer is somewhere in my own head or
heart, waiting to be released when I've reached —
what? Probably, when I have fully come to terms with
the enormity of change in all of the dimensions of life,
physical, mental, emotional, social, spiritual; with the
chaos of loss, then the disjunction of loss and growth,
and finally the emergence of a healed, changed,
accepting man.... Sometimes the only way I cope is by
shortening my frame of reference to now, this minute,
no future, no past. When I've survived this way for a
while, I'm then able to return to the reality that there
was a past, and that "future" is a viable concept.
Slowly, these desperate times diminish, and as I get a
bit better, I'm often then able to face traumas I've put
off, or denied.

*(From the letters of a 64-year-old
widower)*

If you realize loneliness in this way, you may endure a painful self-awareness which, in turn, produces insights and motivates you to make necessary changes in focus or direction; or you may find that such self-awareness causes despair, searching, or immersion in activity. One widower speaks for many when he describes how he avoids the powerful feelings which plague him whenever he is alone and lonely: "I run around. I keep busy. I'm on the go." Of course, running around reduces the risk of confronting any grief-related conditions, not just loneliness.

One of the realizations you may have is that of your own deficiency in areas in which your wife was strong. It is not uncommon for a man to feel that his wife had more compassion or loyalty or was more forgiving or nurturing than he was.

> The last few nights have been white nights because as an aging man, I suffer increasingly from insomnia (as well as introspection). The combination made me suddenly realize that in all my long life I had never done a single thing of which I could be genuinely proud: no act of true courage, generosity, sacrifice, or even pure kindness. It is appalling to contemplate — which I did. After my dear wife, so filled with compassion, love and loyalty had died, there was little encouragement to rectify that terrible lack.
> (C. L. Sulzberger, *How I Committed Suicide*)

If harsh self-examination takes place, you may react in any number of ways. You may temporarily withdraw, seek out the admiration and approval of others, or experience physiological or psychological symptoms.

Experiencing Physiological and Psychological Symptoms

The physical and psychological effects of grief on widowers are very real, and for widowers the physical effects are more pronounced than for widows. Men who are surviving the loss of their wives are prone to experience any of the following:

• Increased visits to physicians

- Increased frequency in illness without consulting a physician
- Use of psychotropic medication
- Severe depression
- Cirhossis of the liver
- Diseases of the heart
- Suppression of the immune system

Beginning in their sixties, most men start to experience a declining energy level and a decrease in their overall capacities. The man in this age bracket or older may have vision or hearing difficulties or some other illness or impairment. The illness and death of a loved one, further reduces such a survivor's capacity to function. There has also been speculation by some researchers that the loss of the marital state takes away more from a man than a woman; that is, that being married is more psychologically advantageous to men than to women.

It is certainly true that when the survivor ignores his feelings and his health, he sets himself up on a debilitiating or self-destructive course. The release of grief, the exploration of conditions and reactions to the loss of a loved one, the interaction with fellow survivors, and the reinvestment of energy in ideas, things, and people will all contribute to better physical and psychological health. The benefits of physical contact with other people — just a touch, a pat, or a hug — have been known to produce distinctly positive physiological reactions, which may include healing. *If you wish to be a survivor who participates in healing himself, you will release your stressful emotions and discuss your grief-related thoughts and conditions.* (See Chapter 8: *Releasing Grief*) You will give and receive affection, respond to love when it is offered, and devote time to taking care of and nourishing your body.

Special Issues of Survival

After your wife's death, there are three special issues which you may confront:

- A changed relationship with your children and other family members

- Social changes

- Dating and remarriage

Changed Relationships with Family

Most widowers do not live with their children or other relatives, receive assistance from children, give assistance to them, or have a wide supportive network of friends or family. In the extreme, they may even experience breaks in family ties.

A men's grief group facilitator pointed up this lack when he discussed men's views on the subject of family. "One of the men in the group had never had children, so one of the things the group talked about a lot was what it was like to have children. The widower without children felt that having children must be a tremendous support to the widowers who were fathers. But, in fact, in a lot of those cases the men's value on their children's support was played down. In a sense, some men did feel some support, but they didn't feel free to depend on their children."

If you find yourself very severely affected by the death of your wife, you may now be concerned about being a burden to your children. You may say, "They have their own lives. I can't expect them to take care of me," or "They have their children to worry about," or their jobs, and so on. Yet at the same time you may actually long to be included in family events, outings, or dinners, or to make more frequent casual visits. You may see yourself as socially isolated and want your family to help fill the gap.

> One realizes that children have their own lives to lead.
> Ours were all adults, the youngest 24 years of age, so
> that although they were concerned for their parent,
> they have their own concerns. At times — and I found
> especially on weekends — I felt very much alone.
> *(From the letters of A. Greenslade)*

You may feel that you never bonded with your children as fully as your wife did. You may even realize that you were often an absent provider-supporter who did not fully participate in all the various facets of child-rearing which bring a parent and child closer together. You might say, "I always felt somewhat like an outsider," or "I never really got that close to the children," or "I'm not good with kids."

Many men feel more in touch with a child's achievements than with a child's character, emotional needs, or propensities. You may believe that you don't possess the skills necessary to communicate with your children, that you don't understand what they require, or that you don't want to appear in need of them.

> When the stress would let up a little bit, then my daughter would say something about how my wife looked when she died, or how she suffered. I'm sure my daughter had to say these things to get it off her chest, but it didn't do me any good. And then, I'd do the same to her. Also, I've never been overly fond of children, and Gloria was just the opposite. She lived for those grandchildren. She was the best mother to our daughter. I'm not that much into kids. I love my daughter dearly, but I didn't have that much to do with raising her because Gloria was so good with her, and I worked.
>
> *(Widower with one grown daughter)*

On the other hand, you may be in the minority of men who do not feel emotionally isolated from their children after the loss of their wives. You may even become increasingly involved in family activities and engage in an open and frequent exchange of affection with your children. Such relationships are very nurturing, but unfortunately, they are not the norm.

Social Changes

As a result of your changed marital status, you'll find yourself in a different social position and with a different outlook. Your social participation and the types of activities you engage in will undergo a transition which may, at first, seem strange.

Generally, the older you are the more difficult it's going to be for you to adapt yourself to a "single" status. Also, if you're not a member of any club or organization and do not belong to a church or other community group, you'll feel more socially isolated.

> Ours is a mobile society so that we do not have the
> same ties to the community that our parents had. In
> our case Kathleen and I had lived in Vancouver for a
> little over 5 years when she became ill. In your sixties
> you do not make friends with anywhere the ease that
> you do when you are 20.
>
> *(From the letters of A. Greenslade)*

In the past you may have relied upon your wife to make social contacts, to connect you with family, friends, and community. Also, you're not likely to have many, if any, male friends in your situation, simply because widows outnumber widowers. Both of these factors enforce your need for companionship and a support group, especially if you're retired.

Robert Rubinstein of the Philadelphia Geriatic Center describes a widower's day: "Involved in a grief life, he participates in a variety of passive, nonsocial activities, such as listening to the all news radio station (famous for its repetition of news items), reading the newspaper, watching TV, looking out the window, and sitting and thinking about the past. He does not have any daily highlights that are truly external in nature.... Rather, he describes his favorite moments of each day as visits from friends and acquaintances, of whom two or three drop by daily, typically for periods of time less than one-half hour."

Any widower who has a tendency toward passive activity can help himself by scheduling and planning activities ahead. By doing so he'll be less likely to become the victim of serious depression or physical incapacitation. He can schedule himself to keep going — not as a way of *avoiding* his grief, but as a way of *accompanying* his grief. He can plan things to do along with the process of grieving.

> One thing I'm doing now is I'm setting up dinner
> dates with lots of people. We go out and of course
> we're not all well-fixed financially so we just go dutch.
> What we really want is, we just want to have each
> other's company.... We set up a purely platonic
> relationship, friend with friend.
>
> *(Retired widower)*

We go together and we have lunch together once a
week. I had him for dinner night before last, and he
has me over there for dinner. He listens and lets me
talk. He is a nice mature person. He's very
understanding, knowledgeable, and receptive.

> *(Widower describing his male friend
> who is also a survivor)*

Understanding and compassionate male companionship can
be extremely valuable to any man during his grieving period —
and on throughout the rest of his life. (See Chapter 11: *Grieving
and Male Companionship*)

Dating and Remarriage

Research has shown that a widower is much more likely
than a widow to develop a new relationship for the purpose of
a marital commitment.

What I miss most and need desperately is to be the
most important person in the world to someone, and
to feel that way myself about someone. I had the
knowledge for 34 years that someone was very special
to me. Now I miss that feeling so very much.

> *(65-year-old widower)*

A widower will date sooner after his spouse's death than
will a widow, but dating for both widowers and widows tends
to increase in the thirteenth month following the spouse's death,
perhaps as a response to the period of initial mourning being
over. Widowers, of course, have more social opportunities and
more marital prospects because of the greater number of widows
in the population. It's also easier for a man to enter into romantic
relationships with a wider age-range of women. In general, widowers have more of a tendency to try to solve emotional, physical, and domestic issues by remarrying.

A man who marries relatively soon after his wife's death will
almost certainly be one who has not gone through a normal
grieving process. His grief will have been inhibited or suppressed
when he turned his mental, emotional, and physical energies to
a new relationship. He will go through the Retreating phase, in-

cluding shock and disbelief, which will then be followed by a short period during which he undergoes real grief-related emotions. Then he appears to experience complete (or nearly complete) recovery when he meets his new partner.

A widower described the response of one of the other recently bereaved men in his grief support group:

> We started out by explaining what our situation was.
> This man couldn't say anything. He just broke down.
> He just cried. That's all he did was cry. He didn't say
> a word. I thought, "My goodness, that man is worse
> off than I am." Then he didn't come back to the group
> for two weeks. So I called him. He said he had found
> someone. He'd only lost his wife two months before. I
> talked to him for a few minutes. He said he had found
> a new love, was alleviating his grief, and he was
> happy. They were going on a cruise.
>
> *(Widower, participant in a Hospice*
> *support group)*

Stories such as this are not uncommon. One of the reasons is that cultural conditions make it extremely easy for a man to find another mate. People are much more anxious to "matchmake" for a single man than they are for a woman. This is perhaps an outcome of society viewing the widowed man as someone who needs caring for, whose loneliness and incompleteness can only be abated by a new partner. This is not nearly as true for widowed women. Society, in general, does not perceive the widow as needing to have a mate. In fact, instead of bringing the widow into social situations for the purposes of alleviating her loneliness and creating opportunities for her to find a partner, it's much more likely that she will not be included in a gathering — especially if it consists of couples. Widows are perceived as more of a social threat than widowers. The extra man at dinner or any other social occasion is not usually threatening to other men. As a result, the widower gets more invitations.

Widowers also do not generally have male companionships which permit and encourage serious emotional exchanges. As a result, widowers have more of an incentive than widows to find a new partner of the opposite sex.

Your own views on dating will be shaped by many factors including your dating experiences before marriage (or during your marriage), the length of your marriage, the type of relationship you had with your wife, and your age at the time of your wife's death. In a men's grief group, participants had varying responses regarding the advisability or even the morality of early dating:

> One of the older men in the group was highly critical initially because one of the younger men was starting to date, to get involved with somebody else fairly quickly after his wife died, and that was like the biggest sin in the world for him. By the end of the group they were fine with each other about that. But at first it was like, "I don't know how you could do that." It was like him saying, "I don't have a context for how that could happen, for how you would feel the openness or freedom to do that." I didn't sense it as blaming or judgmental, but it was more like "I don't understand how you could *think* about that." It was actually good to have both of them in the group because they were at two different ends of the pole. And everyone else was somewhere in between.
>
> *(Men's grief group counselor)*

A man who is not at all interested in remarriage after his grief has subsided is often a man who feels as if his wife was irreplaceable and he's not interested in having "second best." "I was married to the mayor," one widower remarked. "Why would I want to remarry to the file clerk?" Another widower explained, "I had the very finest vintage champagne for years, so now I don't have the slightest interest in warm beer." Often a survivor will believe his commitment to his wife continues after her death. He'll say, "I am married to her forever. I could never have another love. She was the only wife I would ever want to have."

> Everything she did...the way she moved...everything about her was just a joy, a gift. The more precious something is to you, the harder it is to lose it. I'm never in the world going to find anyone like her, and I'm smart enough to know that if I ever do get

involved with anyone I'm not going to be able to make a comparison.

(67-year-old widower)

In a study of bereaved spouses, conducted from 1981 to 1986, researchers (Burks, Lund, Gregg and Bluhm) found that the likelihood of a man remarrying was influenced by income, work, and financial resources. In a group of widowed persons, the typical remarried person was male, sixty-six years of age, had an income which exceeded $20,000 a year and some other sources of financial support, had attended some college or trade school after high school, and was employed full or part time. In the same study, it was found that of survivors who do remarry, the men associated feelings of happiness with mental and physical health while the women associated their happiness to external states, such as living conditions.

Prescriptive Drugs

In your initial period of mourning, you may suffer from sleeplessness, which is one of the most common grief-related physical symptoms. If so, you may ask your doctor for a sedative. However, it is important for prescriptive drugs to be used *only to prevent exhaustion in the case of severe insomnia.*

You should not use drugs to numb or to frequently "calm yourself," especially not at the time of the funeral and during the immediate period of loss. When such use occurs, you're unable to experience the emotions and reactions which are necessary components of the normal grieving process. If you're heavily tranquilized or sedated, you'll have to cope with a delayed reaction to your wife's death, or you'll suppress your emotion altogether over an extended period of time, creating negative effects. As an exception, it's generally appropriate for a survivor to seek professional help and to use prescribed antidepressants to treat a severe clinical depression which is threatening to seriously impair his functioning.

Frequently, a widower will turn to other medications during the grief process, for he may have a variety of physical symptoms — back pain, heart palpitations, headaches, digestive disturbances — that cause distress. Again, it's important for all medications to be monitored and considered with care.

If you're taking prescriptive drugs, you should be entirely aware of what you are taking, what symptoms the medication is supposed to alleviate, what the side effects may be, and whether or not the drug is incompatible with any other medications you're taking. Of course, when you're grieving you're not likely to be focused on the details of your medication. It's a good idea to ask someone else to become acquainted with your prescriptive needs and to help you make a list of what you're supposed to take and when.

For people over aged fifty-five, one of the best unbiased resources to be used for screening the most frequently prescribed medications is *Worst Pills, Best Pills: The Older Adult's Guide To Avoiding Drug-Induced Death Or Illness* which can be ordered from Public Citizen Health Research Group, 2000 P. Street, N.W., Suite 700, Washington D.C. 20036, for $12.00 including postage, or purchased from selected bookstores.

The Tyranny of Grief

Loyal Grief

Some widowers feel they need to continue their grieving process as a way of fully portraying their love. Such a situation makes the successful resolution of a loss impossible. Instead, such a survivor becomes a participant in chronic grief. He believes that if he stops crying, yearning, talking and thinking about his wife, he will have abandoned her. He considers himself "disloyal."

Such a widower needs to recognize that his wife can be cherished in memory, and that a relationship continues in the form of reminiscences and moments of memorial, such as visits to the grave, or certain times of the day or week set aside for paying respects. However, active yearning and pining should abate when this other behavior begins. *A surviving husband should not use suffering as evidence of his love, the depth of the couples' relationship, or the strength of the marital bond.*

The Grief of the "Perfect Marriage"

A husband who grieves a "perfect marriage" may say, "In thirty years, my wife and I never argued, never wanted to be separate, were always loving and supportive of one another." Rarely, if ever, does such an ideal relationship exist. If a couple never disagree in thirty years, it is fairly safe to assume that one partner was suppressing some strong feelings that would have been healthier to express — usually resentment or anger at having to consistently be so "nice," "loving," "warm-hearted," or "flexible."

In situations such as these, there may be a significant amount of anger, guilt, and ambivalence to be worked through by the survivor. Admission of what the marriage really was, examination of all its positive and negative facets, and recall of the whole person will make it possible to work toward successful resolution of a real loss, not a fairytale loss.

The Outlook

If you feel that you are within the majority of widowers who are not generally expressive of their emotions, who intellectualize or suppress their grief, or who avoid thoughts and feelings by keeping busy, you may find yourself focusing more on the disruption and disorder which exists in the practical areas of your life. Your basic needs — meals, house, and clothing — may become paramount. Your sexual concerns may often dominate your thoughts and feelings.

In your effort to find a "solution" for your disrupted state of mind or a quick cure for your aching heart, you may even decide to make some drastic major change, such as sell your house, quit your job, transfer to another city, buy new property, or completely transform your lifestyle. *It is completely unwise to make any such changes for at least one year following your wife's death.* Such crucial decisions require an accurate perspective, a calm approach, and substantial reasons for taking the actions. While you will be better able to assess your proposed plan after the first year of your loss, you may need additional time. If you are thinking of making a significant change, and you feel a great urgency about doing so, then that is all the more reason for you to exercise caution. Allow yourself an adequate time period in which to weigh all the pros and cons and to consult any necessary professional or personal advisors.

To successfully resolve the loss of your wife, you'll need to take your time working it through, experiencing and releasing your grief, and then slowly and gradually reinvesting your energy in new goals, people, projects, and ideas.

The Working Through phase is discussed fully in chapter 8, which provides specific coping strategies and nurturing techniques to help you deal with the entire grief experience and successfully resolve your loss.

7

Experiencing Loss as a Father

*What I have of my children now are two small
boxes of ashes, remnants of the remnants left by
the fire that destroyed their house a couple of
nights later. Their official memorial is two
consecutively numbered files at the Melbourne
Coroner's Court. To write these words makes my
throat close up as if I'm going to choke....
...The best you ever had and the best you ever
gave — both are gone, torn away, blotted out...
Your grief is all you have.*

(JOHN TITTENSOR, *YEAR ONE*)

This chapter discusses some of the most difficult and unique challenges a man often faces as he survives the loss of his child. You may recognize your experience rather prominently in some examples, and not at all in others. This is because the way you respond to your child's death is influenced by a number of factors, particularly the cause of your child's death. For example, an accidental death, suicide or murder will provoke in the surviving father certain kinds of reactions that will not be experienced by a father whose child died of leukemia—and the reverse is also true.

In addition, as you survive your child's death, you'll be likely to find that your response to the loss differs from that of your wife. With some couples, the differences in grief-related reactions and conditions are numerous and extreme; with others, they're less dramatic. So as you survey the various responses which have been identified with grieving fathers (and in some cases, mothers) you will find yourself relating more to some than to others.

- Fathers tend to be private in their grief and reluctant to talk.
- Fathers "keep busy" after the death.
- Fathers are inclined to exhibit more anger and aggression than their wives and to mask their other prominent feelings.
- More frequently, fathers tend to experience the loss of a child as an "emptiness" or "void"; in contrast, mothers more often experience the loss as "missing" and "loneliness."
- Fathers are not inclined to ask for compassion, support, or affection.
- Fathers do not as frequently seek professional help.
- Fathers return to "normal functioning" more quickly than mothers.

When surviving an infant's death:

- Fathers will usually experience less guilt than mothers.
- Fathers' grief reactions are more likely to be of lesser intensity and shorter duration.

The differences which have been reported in regard to mothers' and fathers' grief can be attributed to two factors. The first factor, cultural expectations, has been repeatedly emphasized. The second factor is that men are usually more adept at masking their emotions and — as a natural outcome — may underreport emotional issues and reactions. In addition, the dissimilarities in grief reactions after an infant's death may arise from differing degrees of intensity in the mothers' and fathers' bond with the infant.

Upon the death of a child, most men find themselves functioning in two major roles: Protector and Grief Manager.

The Grieving Father as Protector

Even though you may have been conscious of shielding your family from harm prior to your child's death, that role becomes even more pronounced after the death. You're viewed by others (as well as by yourself) as Protector of the immediate family members, your wife, and surviving children. In some cases, your protection may extend to the child's grandparents and your family friends as well. Especially if you and your wife have lost an infant or young child, you'll be regarded by others as the potential "pillar of strength." *Regardless of whether or not this is true*, you'll either assume, or be thrust into, a leadership role; you'll be the decision-maker who takes care of the business at hand and who does not reveal the scope and depth of his own grief. If, under normal everyday circumstances, you've always been expected to provide, protect, and solve problems, you'll now find those same expectations greatly magnified. As this occurs, your own emotional, mental, and physical needs may be ignored or minimized by others. In an effort to fulfill others' expectations, as well as those you have for yourself, you'll be apt to feel a strong need to suppress your own emotions. Being emotional would make you vulnerable. Being vulnerable would mean you could not adequately protect.

As Protector, you're caught up in two main tasks: making decisions and cushioning the blow.

Making Decisions

You may need to make decisions regarding a variety of procedures, processes, and family actions, including whether or not to permit an autopsy and the type of burial to have for your child. You may have to select the location of the services and determine the degree of involvement of family and clergy. During the initial period, if you're involved in the necessary business of the loss, you may dismiss your heartfelt reactions, keep your grief under wraps, or, as one father put it, "sweep it under the carpet."

Cushioning the Blow

You will serve as a buffer between the actual tragedy and your wife and surviving children. You may, in fact, believe that you need to cushion the blow for everyone who is involved. If so, you may field phone calls, screen inquiries, and intercept visitors. Depending on the nature of the death, you may try to cover up disturbing facts, especially in the case of your child's accidental death, suicide, or homicide. Again, as you assert yourself in this way, your own feelings stay hidden under layers of responsibility and grim determination.

The Bereaved Father as Grief Manager

As a bereaved father, you not only manage your own grief, you may also try to manage others' grief as well. If so, your rationale will be that if you or others do or don't do certain things, the grief of your loved ones will be made easier or shorter.

In Elisabeth Kubler-Ross's *On Children and Death*, she relates the story of a father whose wife was driving the car in which both of the couple's children were killed. As a consequence of the accident, the wife also had her leg amputated. Her husband's hospital visits were very stoic. Kubler-Ross reports, "We saw this father after one of his visits and asked him why he had showed so little emotion. With a surprised look, he explained that he had been explicitly instructed by his wife's doctor not to upset her, not to cry in front of her...not to bring up the issue of the children and amputation. He thought he had done a good job!"

Similarly, you may believe that if you behave with restraint and deal with everything "rationally", you can dilute the pain of others, take "their minds off" the death, and lessen their total grief experience.

In the case of parents whose child dies after a terminal illness, the managing of grief begins *before* the child's death.

Anticipatory Grief

Typically, anticipatory grief follows this general pattern. The parents will:

- Acknowledge the inevitability of their child's death.

- Experience grief-related reactions (anger, confusion, anxiety, fear, and so on).

- Review, reconcile, and compile. This involves looking at the child's life in its whole context, what it has been in the past, its unique characteristics; reconciling oneself to the death; compiling and stowing away in memory things the child said or did, the way he or she looked at a certain moment. (It may also involve keeping the child's notes and drawings or making an audio or video of the child.)

- Detach. Parents allow an emotional distance (which will range from very slight to quite pronounced) to grow between the self and child. Detachment is not necessarily externally revealed, but internally experienced.

Fathers can be involved in anticipatory grief to the same extent as mothers. Generally, though, the mother will spend more time with the terminally ill child, and, as a result, she will reach a point at which she is willing to let the child go earlier than will the father. As a professional counselor at a children's hospital explained, "The intensity of that experience and the time spent with the child allow the mother to see that the body the child is in is just not going to last; it's not worth trying to hang on to the dying child. The father, on the other hand, who spends less time with the child, may be removed enough from the situation that he'll try to hang on longer. He'll take a longer time to accept the inevitable before he goes through the detachment process."

In such cases, a father may try to manage his grief by delaying it, holding onto the child longer, or being unrealistically hopeful in the face of futility.

Masking Feelings

Nowhere in all the annals of sex discrimination is there a more glaring injustice than that thrust upon a bereaved father.

My husband was a victim.

Here was a man, a father, who watched his child

being buried and according to convention was asked
by society to "keep a stiff upper lip."
(Harriet Schiff, The Bereaved
Parent)

As noted in previous chapters, the cultural expectations for men
are changing, but, as yet, they haven't changed to a great degree.
Unfortunately, in far too many cases, a bereaved father still believes he must keep it all "stuffed down."

> I have never had an emotional breakdown over it
> where I could just get down on my knees and sob. I
> feel as if I still need to do that.
> (Father whose 4-year-old son died
of leukemia.)

Sadness, fear, anxiety, and loneliness are the feelings that
most often go "under wraps." Anger, aggression, and action are
more easily displayed, since they are the more "expected" reactions of men.

> My husband's way of dealing with it was to go out
> and build a woodshed. Then, when everyone left, he
> went back to work.
> (Mother survivor of a neonatal
death)

Closely linked to this suppression of emotion is the father's
reluctance to seek support from others, to attend a grief group,
or to avail himself of professional help if he needs it. The message
he gets from others is that he won't be expressive, emotional, or
needy.

In Recovering From the Loss of a Child, by Katherine Anne
Donnelly, a bereaved father states: "Most people, even friends,
will call and never ask me how I am doing. They ask how Angela
is. It's as if my wife is supposed to have a reaction to the loss of
our child, but I am not, and I find it drives me bananas — that
you are a man and not supposed to be upset with these things.
It's not viewed as the same loss."

Some men find it easier to accept this type of treatment than
others. But when it comes to masking feelings, many bereaved
fathers have to continually battle themselves.

It's such a hard pain I feel, that knife in the chest, and
I have to harden myself against it, clenching my fists
until my body is so taut and hard it trembles all over,
clenching my teeth hard until my head shakes so much
I can't see properly. And being hard with myself in a
different way in front of other people because I don't
want to keep burdening them with this awful
continuous preoccupation with my own loss.

(John Tittensor, Year One)

When you're surviving the loss of your child you'll have
your own individual perspectives and anxieties regarding your
public behavior. Many grieving fathers have expressed one or
more of the following concerns:

- I don't feel confident about how to respond as a grief-stricken father.

- People are watching me to see how I'll act.

- Friends seem to be ignoring the death or avoiding me because of the death.

A father whose child who died of leukemia echoed the
thoughts of many bereaved men when he talked about the responses he most appreciated from co-workers and social acquaintances following his son's death.

It takes integrity and guts to walk up and
acknowledge something that is a major portion of
somebody's life. Nothing meant more to me than
someone acknowledging what had happened because,
for the most part, people would rather talk about
almost anything else.

The awkwardness that other people feel may frequently be
a burden for you and your wife. You may find that as you mask
your own emotions in public and social situations, you'll be feeling some resentment and anger or discomfort and uncertainty
toward those who expect you to suppress your feelings.

It was almost as if they [co-workers, friends and
acquaintances] had programmed themselves to go

through a certain expression. It had to do with body
language. It had to do with facial expression. It had to
do also with what was said. It was almost as
though...and I'm sure they were very genuine about
their feelings...but it was almost as though it was an
ungenuine thing I was perceiving. That's not because
they were. It's because that is the way I was perceiving
of it at that time. I was going through a lot of changes.

> (*Father who survived the loss of his
> teenager to suicide*)

In the first year following the death of his children, a grieving father made the following observation:

Changes I notice in myself: less confident among
strangers — sometimes even with people I know well;
my voice begins to shake, I lose the thread of a
perfectly ordinary conversation; or, quite often, I can
think of nothing to say at all and come up with
laborious cliches or irrelevancies — sometimes in a
voice which does not seem to be my own.

> (John Tittensor, *Year One*)

In addition to the severe pain of the loss, it's possible that
your child's death may produce in you some feelings of guilt and
ambivalence, as well as negative physiological effects.

Guilt

There are as many specific guilts as there are individual survivors.
As you grieve your child's death, there may be times when you
blame yourself in any one of the following ways:

- I was not protective enough.

- I did not love enough.

- I did not pay adequate attention to what was going on in
  my child's life.

- I took our child to the wrong doctor or hospital or permitted a harmful treatment or medication.

- I shouldn't have been away from home.

- I should have been able to anticipate the death and stop it.

- I was too preoccupied with concerns about myself, my business, and my needs.

- I'm being punished for something I thought or did.

- I tried everything I could to save our child, but I wasn't good enough, strong enough, or smart enough.

- I shouldn't have gotten a divorce and left the family.

If you're suffering from such self-inflicted blame, it's important to remember that very rarely does any guilt, no matter how strong it is, have a solid, logical base. Most guilts are disputable. They arise from the need to blame something or someone for your child's death, so you blame yourself. But if there is some real, legitimate reason for guilt (such as leaving a two-year-old unattended next to a swimming pool), it is absolutely necessary for the guilt to be worked through. A tragic error in judgement cannot be relived and corrected, *but it can be forgiven and let go.* (See the discussion on releasing feelings in chapter 8.)

Ambivalence

Sometimes a father will report that, prior to the death, he felt some degree of ambivalence toward his child. Perhaps his son or daughter did not carry out the father's dreams, did not share the father's belief system, did not do well in school, or stay out of trouble, or have as close a relationship with the father as with the mother.

In fact, the father may have felt resentful because the child was the mother's top priority, taking a large portion of her attention and absorbing her affection and love. *Feelings of ambivalence are a natural, inevitable part of most close human relationships.* A father's relationship with his child is not sacrosanct in this respect. Ambivalence, of course, is not something a parent feels he can discuss easily with others. But feelings like these are real, and he should not ignore them. They are as important, or perhaps more important, than any of his other grief-related reactions, and if they're not confronted may result in unresolved grief. This, of course, makes healthy recovery impossible.

Deteriorating Health

A group facilitator for a couples' grief group observed that "Many of the men don't take care of themselves. Their covert behavior is to let themselves go. They let their health deteriorate."

There is a tendency for grief to turn inward with men, and take its toll, especially with the use of alcohol or other self-destructive behavior, such as driving oneself unrelentlessly or getting involved in life-threatening situations. Men who follow this type of course appear to "get over their grief" quickly; but, in reality, their grief is merely transformed into something else which is ultimately harmful.

A mother commented on this syndrome when she described the behavior of her ex-husband after the accidental death of the couple's teenaged son.

> He drinks. He runs away. He's getting rid of old friends, leaving his present location. His whole life is going through a transition. He kind of walked away from everything.

Father's who react this way are reluctant to communicate or, in extreme cases, will *refuse* to communicate with anyone who threatens to get behind the mask.

Special Effects of Infant Loss

After the death of an infant, a woman usually has more thoughts about her dead child than her husband does. She also has more visions, dreams or fantasies. She may experience more sleep disturbances and will be likely to suffer from more anxiety and depression as a result of the death. Generally, her grief continues for a longer period of time. She will often have a strong need to talk about it to her husband — frequently and at length. While her husband may sit and listen, or participate in a verbal exchange within the first few weeks or so after their child's death, he will not want to continue to talk about it as long as she will.

> I'd say I needed to talk about it, and he would try to understand, but he just couldn't talk about it. We grieved very differently and we came to a point where we accepted that. He accepted what I finally needed to do, and if I couldn't get it from him then he felt it was okay to get it from a support group.
>
> *(Wife who survived a neonatal death)*

It is necessary to stress that this type of reaction is not always the case. It is *usually* the case. A father may have more intense grief and a longer grieving period than the mother following their infant's death; but the majority of fathers will be more likely to exhibit intense grief after the death of a school-age child who has been less exclusively under the care of the mother.

Even though mothers' guilts are greater after the death of an infant and cause prolonged suffering, fathers have guilt feelings as well. A father may feel guilty for urging his wife to get pregnant, having been responsible for her getting pregnant, having sex during pregnancy, or being unsolicitious in regard to her health and sense of well-being during her pregnancy. While a mother will often have feelings of being "defective" or "less womanly" after her infant's death, the father, too, can feel inadequate, as if the two of them were unable to fulfill a normal expectation.

It should be noted that a father who undergoes the death of any ill child, but particularly his infant, may frequently feel that he is overlooked, ignored, or dismissed at the hospital. People will not solicit his feelings, nor will they offer much, if any, comfort. A pat on the shoulder from a caring professional may be the extent of support a grieving father receives.

In the case of neonatal death, a father may need to see the burial through to its conclusion while his wife is still in the hospital. In such a case, he'll be overseeing his child's death and his wife's hospital care at the same time. As a consequence, he won't have an opportunity to share his grief with his wife.

The Communication Gap

As noted earlier, you may find it difficult to share your emotional feelings and reactions after the loss of your child for fear of intensifying your wife's grief, keeping it going for a longer duration, or reminding her of a past you believe is better left forgotten.

> I wanted to talk, but I was afraid to. I thought she couldn't handle it, or that it would make her feel worse. I just kept shoving it all down, saying nothing. Nothing at all.
>
> *(34-year-old father, survivor of a teenaged daughter's accidental death)*

You and your wife will probably be more likely to share feelings of anger or hostility regarding the unfairness of your child's death, or the actions or neglect of certain family members following your child's death, or your treatment by members of the medical profession. You'll have greater differences in the expression of your fear and sadness — the emotions which strike closest to the pain of the loss and which reflect a greater vulnerability.

> It's very difficult for a husband and wife to talk about these things. It really is. Because the hurt is so deep. So you do it in your own way, you see. And women deal with it far differently than men do, I think.
>
> *(Father of a murder victim)*

In a study conducted with the parents of 50 adolescents who had attempted suicide, researcher Jerry Jacobs noted that "there was a general reluctance among fathers to participate in the study." In fact, only two fathers participated. Consequently, the majority of interviews were done with the mothers.

This type of reaction among fathers is not confined to suicide-related grief. It reflects the general reponses of fathers who survive other types of deaths as well. They are less likely to communicate with outsiders such as social workers, counselors, clergy, or researchers. However, *once a man's initial reluctance is overcome,* he feels relieved and is pleased to have, as one survivor put it, "lifted the cement cloud from around my head and heart."

If a father doesn't share his thoughts and emotions, and conveys the message to his wife that he believes her need to talk about their child's death is obsessive ("dwelling on it"), morbid, or self-indulgent, then the communication gap between them will broaden, and the grief process will become an even more intensely disturbing experience for both of them.

> Here is something major that we have experienced together, and I feel we should be able to share, but Z doesn't want to talk about it, or deal with it...Z reacts to stress the way that he has always reacted to stress in his life...I've lost all respect and love for him and have built up a brick wall that I don't plan to let down.
> (Quoted in Klass, "Marriage and Divorce Among Bereaved Parents In A Self Help Group," *Omega*)

If you work full time and your wife works part time or is at home during the day, you'll be likely to go through the initial grieving periods in very different ways. For example, if you've been required to return to work after your child's death (either because of your company's policy, or economic need), or you've chosen to return to work as a way of getting through this painful period, you'll have many more distractions and more stimulation than your wife. Your required interactions with other people, along with your job-related responsibilities and stresses, will demand your attention and performance, making it less possible for you to concentrate exclusively on your loss.

> I went to work the day after he died. I know some people thought it strange, but it was good for me. It kept my thoughts away from what had happened. If I had had to stay at home, I would have found some work there. It helps me to use my hands.
> (Survivor of a neonatal death, quoted in Dyregrov and Mattheisen, "Similarities and differences in mothers' and father's grief following the death of an infant," *The Scandanavian Journal of Psychology*)

Often a husband will report that his wife's circumstances after the death allowed her to vent her feelings more freely, or she actually arranged to have time to herself so she could grieve. As a result, she had more mental and emotional space in which to miss, yearn for, or have visions of your child, to relive scenes, or to think about the death. Some husbands saw this behavior as "brooding" or being "obsessive." In such circumstances a husband may project a silent or more overt message that says, "Let's move on. Let's get over this." His wife on the other hand may see his message as "Let's not feel."

Even if you and your wife prefer to stay at home rather than return to work after your child's funeral, you'll probably force yourselves to go back; but both of you may experience some difficulty performing on the job. For example, you may have demands made on you when your mind is preoccupied and you'll have to force yourself to focus your thoughts on your job when you're actually thinking about the way you feel. One father reported his "total lack of concentration" after his teenaged son was killed in an automobile accident. "My memory," the father explained, "went from excellent to very poor." As a result he took to carrying a pad and pencil in his shirt pocket. "My brain," he would say, patting his pocket. "Without it, I can't remember a thing."

Men who are surviving the loss of a child repeatedly make the point that employers should be more cognizant of what grief entails. "They could make the initial grieving period easier by allowing a man a longer bereavement leave," suggested the father of an eight-year-old cancer victim. (Most men will have only three days.) When a grieving father does return to work, the employer should recognize that the father's concentration and sleeping pattern have both been temporarily affected. As a result, allowances should be made whenever possible. A man who is coping with the effects of grieving should not be expected to work at an optimum level. Women who work full-time (including many divorced mothers) will have the same strenuous pressures, though co-workers and employers will generally be more solicitous and understanding when a woman is grieving the loss of her child.

When the work requirements and social situations of the mother and father differ, and when extreme communication gaps do exist, distancing between the spouses inevitably occurs. As the husband and wife withdraw from one another and create their own individual worlds, their tensions mount, the physical as well as emotional distances increase, and estrangement is the result.

Distancing and Marital Difficulties Among Grieving Parents

A number of issues and situations which arise with grieving parents can exacerbate an already strained marriage, or cause difficulties in a marriage that was previously satisfactory or successful.

> We were very close during the time that Jeff was in the hospital. We've never been so close in our entire lives. We talked, we shared. Then when it was over, it was over, and so was the closeness. So it was a double loss.
>
> *(Wife, survivor of neonatal death)*

When you and your wife no longer need to function as one unit, you may find yourselves making a rapid adjustment. That is, as a bereaved parent you may have been one-half of a close supportive team who shared a tragedy; now you are two separate individuals. This adjustment is more pronounced if you have lost an only child.

Within the first year or so after the death, you and your wife will be forced to make a transition from one mode of behavior to another. For example, if you were a tightly bound pair who had a third person as your focus — your dead or dying child — now you must shift your focus toward each other, your surviving children, or yourselves.

Regardless of the specific changes in dynamics which may occur in your marriage, one outcome is certain: your relationship will not be the same as it was prior to your child's death. It may grow stronger. It may have a different emphasis, direction, or quality. Or it may deteriorate. Being aware of the major factors which are influencing your relationship can be the first step toward preventing a poor outcome.

The situations which you and your wife may experience after your child's death are likely to include one of more of the following:

- Differing intimacy and sexual needs

- Differing views about having other children

- Disagreements about methods of child rearing to be used for the surviving child or children

- The end of a "truce" which had been called for the sake of the dying child, or until the initial grieving period was over

- Dramatic effects of a sudden or violent death

- Negative reactions to your spouse's presence, activities, or beliefs

Differing Intimacy and Sexual Needs

The needs and desires which relate to intimacy and sex constitute a potential hazard to the marital relationship of any grieving couple. One partner may feel more inclined toward affection, tenderness, and verbal expressions of love, but not be interested in complete sexual intimacy. The other partner may have strong drives for sexual intimacy and feel rejected when those drives are not satisfied.

You or your wife may feel that participating in sex is morally wrong, lacking in respect for your dead loved one, too demanding physically, or simply a marital "task" that offers no personal fulfillment or pleasure.

If you engage in sexual intimacy, you may experience one or more of several reactions. You may feel that sex provides (1) a direct line to your deepest emotions (which may include an unleashing of feelings that seem overpowering, startling, or disturbing), (2) a sense of mental, emotional and physical relief, (3) an enjoyable "intermission" during an otherwise intense and painful time, or (4) an opportunity to generate new life, to conceive or cause conception.

Most importantly, if both you and your wife are responsive, the act of making love can affirm your devotion, aliveness, and closeness, as well as your ability to create and enjoy a positive pleasurable experience together. It also provides the opportunity for you to reciprocate to one another through gestures, caresses, and words, and by so doing enrich your existing bond.

There is no "decent" time period which should be observed before resuming your sexual relationship. It isn't necessary for you or your wife to deprive yourself of pleasure in order to prove your love for your child who has died. Instead, you'll need to reestablish an intimacy that is emotionally, mentally, and physically satisfying to both of you. Doing so requires patience, understanding, and adjustment. When sexual relationships undergo change as a result of disinterest, lack of physical energy, preoccupation, or depression, it may take a considerable amount of time for the two of you to make readjustments. In fact, it's not uncommon for a marital sexual relationship to be inhibited or otherwise changed for two or three years following a child's death.

Differing Views About Having Other Children

If you and your wife have lost an only child, the decision about whether or not to have another child is a major one, and may have a dramatic resolution. For example, in a study of women who had survived the loss of a stillborn child, 50 percent of them decided against future pregnancies and half of that group underwent sterilization procedures. Such decisions, of course, can cause a great deal of conflict if you and your wife are not in agreement.

Conflict can also arise in a marriage in which the husband has children from a former marriage. In such a case he may not wish to subject his second marriage to the trial of another possible loss and he may not pursue having additional children.

Each father, of course, will have his own response to his situation, depending upon a variety of other factors which are at work in his marriage. Generally, however, a disagreement about raising a family can be the source of serious dissension and may permanently alter a marital relationship.

Disagreements About Methods of Child Rearing

Following the death of a child, it isn't uncommon for one or both parents to be overprotective of their surviving children. Parents' priorities, perspectives and concerns change due to the loss of a child. The father may feel that the surviving child is garnering too much of the mother's attention, leaving little time left over for himself, or the mother may feel that the father is stifling the social development of a surviving teenager after a sibling's death. If the child-rearing practices of the two parents do not coincide, a conflict will result.

Stresses can arise, too, if the remaining children believe that the parents loved the dead child more than them. Feelings like these create additional tension in a household that may already be severely disordered and emotionally chaotic.

The End of a Marital "Truce"

The divorce rate among bereaved parents is relatively high. Parents who divorce after the death of a son or daughter have usually experienced marital difficulties prior to the death of their child.

Parents who had divorced before the death of their child may find themselves attempting to reestablish a relationship that may have been minimal, superficial, or even totally abandoned.

Couples who were already heading toward separation or who were, as one husband put it, "estranged, but still living under one roof" frequently call a silent (or not-so-silent) truce when they are faced with the terminal illness of a child. They begin to operate as a unit so they may deal with the medical world, ease their child's hospitalization, divide visitation times, or share the child's transportation to and from labs, clinics, or hospitals. They may stay together so the child will be the recipient of certain medical benefits or insurance policies.

As researcher Dennis Klass observes, "there is not a simple relationship between parental bereavement and divorce. Marriages don't die with the death of a child, but often they receive an overdue burial.... The death of a child seems to cause parents to examine the whole of their life. Since they have had to stand the pain of the loss of the rich and full relationship to the child, so the pain of losing the withered relationship to the spouse is seen in a different perspective."

Dramatic Effects of a Sudden or Violent Death

When a death is the result of suicide or homicide, nearly every aspect of the marital relationship and family situation undergoes marked change. Family and business routines are drastically altered and social associations are severely strained; intrusions from police, media, or medical personnel may disrupt any semblance of order to which the bereaved parents attempt to cling.

A father reflected on the ways in which he, his wife, and a surviving daughter grieved after the suicide of a teenaged daughter.

> All three of us expressed entirely different griefs. We expressed totally different emotions and they came from different sources. They didn't *mean* the same things. We all talked about it...My wife had done most of her grieving three years before. She had felt that at that time there was nothing more that she could do. With my wife, her grief was more a combination of griefs. And in a way, it was expressed somewhat differently, too, because it had a different pattern to it.

One couple's twenty-one-year-old daughter disappeared after her car ran out of gas on a busy northern California highway. Search parties combed the adjacent mountains for almost three weeks before the young woman's body was finally found, bludgeoned to death in a ravine. The couple spent a year trying to find the killer. Then, at about the end of the second year, they separated. The mother had a "breakdown." The father, who had been determined to seek revenge, finally quit letting his search for the killer consume his life. "I only do it now when I deliberately want to do it. That person was controlling my life." As he found himself regaining control of his life, his marriage disintegrated. "We just weren't compatible any more," he said four years after the killing. "She's still grieving."

This case is similar to many others. Surviving the loss of a murdered child is one of the cruelest tests of human endurance and sanity a parent can experience. To remain sane and alive under such circumstances is an accomplishment. It's important to note that the mother who was described above as "still grieving" after four years is more the norm among survivors of a murder than she is the exception. The grief of the surviving parent is fed by a variety of punishing circumstances and procedures, including extremely lengthy judicial processes which often constitute a form of emotional torture, and recurring violent images which continue to haunt the parents throughout their lives.

Negative Reactions To Your Spouse's Presence, Activities, or Beliefs

One of the least discussed issues following the death of a child has to do with a spouse's *presence* serving as a painful reminder of the deceased. "I love my husband dearly," the wife of an Air Force colonel said, "but sometimes looking at him causes me to have a sudden, small shock, like an electric jolt. Our son looked just like him, walked like him — everything."

There is no cure for such small shocks, except the passage of time. Eventually, seeing the same physical characteristics and mannerisms in a partner will produce a less pronounced response. One parent or the other may continue to be "a living reminder," but the similarities to the dead child will eventually be endurable.

The differing activities of a grieving mother and father may also cause negative reactions. One may keep busy while the other grieves. One may prefer to work, while the other finds even the smallest task overwhelming. One may respond to outsiders or, in the case of a death which is featured in the news, may give interviews and answer public requests. The other may withdraw, seek solitary situations, and eschew any investigation or publicity connected to the death.

Preexisting differences in beliefs will become more apparent following the death. In fact, it's quite possible for the belief system of a husband or wife to change entirely. For example, one partner may begin to attend church and seek solace in religious literature. The other partner may question religion, lose faith, and then turn away from it entirely after the child's death. One partner may believe that it's best to dispose of the child's clothing, belongings, and photographs, while the other partner finds great comfort in having them to touch, hold, or speak to. (A woman who has lost a child often finds solace in handling and looking at her child's belongings. A man is more likely to engage in this behavior when he is grieving the death of his wife.)

Losing The Legacy

> One of my early thoughts was that my wife and I
> would have no grandchildren. There would be no
> passing on of either tangibles or intangibles....
>
> I have been surprised by how the assumptions that a
> man's child will marry and have children — and that
> they will all outlive him — are his constant
> companions molding thought and actions in
> innumerable subtle ways. Suddenly, my thoughts and
> actions were inappropriate because the assumptions on
> which they were based were no longer valid. Until
> some new assumptions replace those shattered by
> Paul's fall, I feel like a ship without engine, sail or
> rudder, floating helplessly without direction.
>
> (Albert F. Knight, "The Death of
> a Son," *New York Times Magazine*)

When you lose your son or daughter, you lose a part of
yourself, a part of your physical body. You lose your connection
to the future, and some of your own qualities and traits disappear. In that respect, your continuity was embodied in your child.
You may even have recognized in your child some of the talents
you most valued in yourself, and felt deep personal pride as you
watched your child grow and mature.

> For each of us, grief is an individual emotion, varying
> from person to person. I have come to the conclusion
> that my grief is a selfish emotion. I grieve because of
> being deprived of Paul's companionship, of being
> deprived of sharing with him our recent tour of the
> European World War II battlefields, of being deprived
> of grandchildren, of being deprived of the task of
> helping Paul find his niche in the world. I grieve, not
> for Paul, but for the loss of the pleasures I think his
> life would have brought me and my wife.
>
> (Albert F. Knight, "The Death of
> a Son," *New York Times Magazine*)

It is difficult to accept that the experiences you anticipated sharing with your child are no longer possible. The promised years of your child's life have been taken away. It's almost as if the years had been allotted to you and your child, and then they were suddenly retrieved.

Finding a Support Group

As will be discussed in chapter 9, sharing your grief with others who have had a similar loss can be extremely beneficial. This is particularly true in the case of bereaved parents. Sharing the loss of a child with others who are going through the same experience is, more often than not, one of the major ways in which you and your wife can facilitate your understanding of one another, open up new avenues of communication, and gain support and energy from trusted outside sources.

Group participation helps to break down feelings of isolation and allows you to see your own and your wife's reactions in the context of others' grief. It allows you to compare your situation to theirs, to identify similar reactions and issues, and to gain insight about coping and nurturing techiniques, as well as other positive experiences.

Participating in a group will make it possible for you to establish new friendships with people who have gone through the same devastating experience. Couples who meet in such a group have the advantage of being informed and knowledgeable about the most important event of one another's lives. Most importantly, perhaps, is the fact that couples who are themselves experiencing the loss of a child will not have difficulty talking about the death's effects. There will be no artificial chatter designed to mask the actuality of the loss and ignore the emotional pain which exists.

Support groups exist throughout the U.S. for the survivors of specific kinds of children's death, such as neonatal death, SIDS, cancer, suicide, or murder. Such a group can be located by contacting local mental health agencies, the social services department or pastoral care office of a large hospital in your region, a nearby hospice or victim service organizations. (Support group procedures, dynamics, and benefits are further discussed in chapter 9.)

8

Releasing Grief

I could have been helped by somebody trying to get me to talk about it, by trying to bring my inner problems out so I could deal with them constructively. Nobody did that. So that type of thing starts to become more and more deep seated. I just kind of ignored it almost, because it was so intense.

(40-YEAR-OLD SURVIVOR OF
VIETNAM CASUALTIES)

As you work to successfully resolve your loss, it's important to recognize that you must first have a complete grieving process. It's not enough to experience the edge of the grieving process, or to undergo the beginning and end of the process. While it may appear to be possible for you to continue your life unchanged after your loved one's death, eventually something is going to give.

When any survivor's grief is inhibited, delayed or absent, some aspect of his or her life is negatively affected. For example, such a survivor, regardless of gender, is more prone to have an impaired immune-system response, depression, and sleep, appetite, and weight disturbances, as well as an increased mortality risk. With some survivors there will also be a tendency toward drug or alcohol dependence, antisocial behavior, delinquent activity, or sexual dysfunction.

The reason for processing grief is not to weaken life, but to strengthen it. While the experience of grief is debilitating at the time, such a condition is temporary. To express normal grief —

grief that is not inhibited, delayed or distorted in some way — is to work toward a positive life. It makes possible healthful living, instead of a diminished, struggling existence. In fact, grief that is *not* dealt with may very well be debilitating for the rest of the survivor's life.

As you confront your own loss and begin to work it through, you can assist yourself by:

- Recognizing any aspects of traditional male behavior which may be detrimental to your grieving process.

- Recognizing debilitating conditions.

- Acknowledging and allowing yourself to experience the entire range of your grief-related emotions.

- Communicating your thoughts, concerns, feelings and conditions.

- Releasing your tears.

Grief is a *process* that occurs within a *life*. Consideration must be given to the survivor's total life context, with all of its challenges, proscriptions, penalties, and rewards. For most men, that context includes some elements of traditional male behavior, many of which are essential to conducting a workable, effective life. But there are also elements which directly *limit* how a man can traverse one of the most profound and challenging human experiences — the loss of his wife, daughter, son, sibling, father, mother, lover, or friend.

Let's consider now the aspects of traditional male behavior which may possibly limit, to some degree, the ways in which you can effectively grieve your loss.

Recognizing Aspects of Traditional Male Behavior

In *The Male Sex Role: Our Culture's Blueprint of Manhood and What It's Done for Us Lately*, Robert Brannon states, "I have gradually come to realize that I, with every other man I know have been limited and diverted from whatever our real potential might have been by the pre-fabricated mold of the male sex role." To find a new approach which can serve you well when dealing with the loss of your loved one consider that you may have *untapped potentials* and *alternative ways* of coping with a major emotional crisis.

Some survivors feel that part of the "real potential" that they have lost is that of fully experiencing emotional events. Such limitations make it necessary for them to live an isolated emotional existence and to be constantly wary of exposure or self-disclosure.

Generally, a man finds it easier to relate to other people and interact with them if he can view them according to their category or function, rather than their needs or feelings. This predisposition is intensified by our social system, which actually discourages compassion. What once was man's pure impulse to reduce the suffering of another human being (for that is man's *instinctive* response) has been replaced with a guardedness in which kindness is often viewed as weakness. We are all exposed to this indoctrination to varying degrees. Western industrial civilization does not generally encourage or require us to identify with the suffering of others. In fact, it often seems as if we are supposed to feel no human connection at all for some segments of society.

This socially endorsed lack of empathy leads to a socially endorsed lack of other feelings as well. Tough mindedness, self-denial, and detachment have long been valued conditions in men's behavior because such conditions make possible an analysis of functions, things, and business transactions. The machine-like qualities of life are emphasized and reinforced — sometimes even to the point of *glorifying* the repression of feeling.

If a man can stay detached, he need not wrestle with feelings which have no comfortable or acceptable place in his life. But once the limitations of detachment are challenged, a whole host of expressions, gestures, and enriching interactions can be realized. Men survivors agree that it is both frightening and freeing to *relinquish the limiting and constricting aspects of their behavior.*

A fifty-nine-year-old novelist and poet described how he felt when he recognized some of the limiting elements within the role he was playing.

> It wasn't until I got into therapy that I realized what
> an incredible influence the movies had on me. That
> was the real educator for me, not school. School almost

got in the way. I learned how to behave as a man. I
identified with Humphrey Bogart, Ray Milland and
John Wayne, and all those people. I bought all that. I
didn't know I was buying it, but I *bought* it all. The
movies when I was growing up were like TV is today
for people. We went to movies to socialize, to meet
girls, to be with male friends. To sit in a row and be
very funny or cool, or make comments.... And I never
realized it but I didn't want to be one of those
supporting players who asked for help or showed that
they were weak or cried. I was like Bogart. Bogart
never told anybody what was going on. He always
offered help. Always had a solution. Then I had to
find out that I was a real human being...and had to
find out...what am I all *about*? What really makes me
work? What makes me tick?

Of course, the media heroes who are today's role models for
boys and men are not Bogart, Milland, nor Wayne. They have different names. But the same general behavior — macho, in control,
aloof — still dominates the movie and TV screen. In fact, such influence appears to be even more pervasive than it was in Bogart's
day. Now we have more rage, more hard-core violence, and more
use of distorted power.

Recognizing Debilitating Conditions

While survivors of both genders are prone to certain debilitating
physical and emotional conditions, in men this susceptibility can
be compounded by the increase in stress which results from always having to maintain control. Regardless of how debilitating
his circumstances might be, the "real man" carries on with the
good fight, plays the game regardless of the injury, and ignores
the pain. He refuses to acknowledge signals of emotional distress
or spiritual injury that may cry out for attention. The learned
message is "Go on with the game," "Tough it out," and "Be hard
nosed." Show them you can win against great odds — that even
death won't get you down.

Masculinity is linked with the capacity to bear discomfort
and pain. It can't be denied that such a capacity has its benefits
and uses in situations which require hard physical labor and

great strength, such as deprived circumstances, performance under pressure, or combat. But the detrimental effects are also fearfully real. When a man ignores adverse bodily conditions, those conditions can deteriorate until they necessitate more prolonged periods of care. For example, the average duration of a man's hospital stay is at least 15 percent longer than that of a woman. In addition, men's mortality rate is higher for most major illnesses. Repeated denial of emotional pain can lead to anxiety, obsessive behavior, and withdrawal, as well as ulcers and back problems.

Though these disturbances and disorders are often simply the result of living in accordance with societal expectations and pressures, the situation is not permanent and irreversible. Positive changes are entirely possible. They occur when the limiting and detrimental effects of behavior are seen for what they are — imprisonments of the emotional and spiritual self which make it impossible to experience the whole range of conditions comprising a full human life.

> Manhood is what we look forward to when we are
> powerless boys and what we look back on with pride
> when we are limping toward the grave. To be known
> as a good man is the highest compliment for a man. It
> is what men despair of achieving when depressed — in
> our careers, our family life, in our sexuality, in our
> values. Our idea of manhood is our motivation toward
> self-respect. And most of us could not be more aware
> that the old images of manhood need revision....
> (Stephen Shapiro, *Manhood*)

Obviously, one of the images of manhood that needs revision for the purpose of processing grief is that of the detached, unemotional male.

Acknowledging the Entire Range of Your Emotions

An anecdote cited in chapter 2 told of the reactions of the male participants in a couples' group in the midwest. When the men were asked to write about their feelings, five of the eight men insisted they had *no* feelings whatsoever. It would be a relief to think that this was a unique belief suffered by a few men in a certain geographical region. Unfortunately, this is not the case.

It was also mentioned earlier that a number of the men who were interviewed regarding the loss of their loved one were reluctant to answer or avoided the question entirely when asked, "What do you fear most?" Some of the men contended that they didn't understand the question, or didn't understand what fear meant, or didn't fear anything. It is highly unlikely that there are a significant number of people (of either sex) who fear nothing at all.

For example, some typical fears which may play a part in keeping the lid on your grief-related emotions are:

- The fear of being vulnerable

- The fear of being misunderstood

- The fear of hurting other survivors

- The fear of losing the respect or admiration of others

- The fear of losing control (of your plans, your body, your mind)

Just as fear can remain unacknowledged, so can a wider range of emotions. To open up your grieving process, to have it follow a healthful course, it's necessary to recognize the total range and intensity of your feelings and emotional conditions. The processing of your grief will run the whole gamut, including any feeling or condition which results from your loss, such as longing or yearning for your loved one, sadness, a need for affection, loneliness, despair, guilt, fear, frustration, confusion, and vulnerability. When the entire realm of your most powerful grief-related reactions is not acknowledged, then your loss is almost certain to remain unresolved.

Tim, a thirty-two-year-old publisher, explained how the loss of an older male friend brought up the earlier, unresolved loss of Tim's father.

> When my close friend died, I'd been suppressing it,
> not letting it get to me overtly. I went in and tried to
> work and came outside after a short while and felt

pressure growing. I broke down and just started blubbering and I was saying "I'm just a kid. I don't know what to do. He [the friend who had died] always knew what to do, but I don't know what to do." And I know that was going back to the loss of my father.

Any man who has not previously acknowledged feelings, or who has only acknowledged certain "male-permitted ones," such as anger or frustration, will be disconcerted by the revelation that, while grieving, a whole keyboard of emotions exists to be played.

What bothered me a lot was the fact that some of these feelings hang on for so long. Once I opened up for the first time, whenever I talked about the same thing, the feelings would well up again and repeat. I got sick and tired...when is it going to *end*? And then, finally, it did end.

(72-year-old, retired engineer)

Michael, a thirty-four-year-old counselor whose father died, explained that because he was in charge of taking care of things, he intentionally delayed his grief.

Michael:	At that time, there was a sense that my sadness was going to be debilitating and that I would not be able to do what I needed to do.
Interviewer:	Was it debilitating?
Michael:	I think my sadness has always been very *freeing*. My *belief* is that it is debilitating.
Interviewer:	The fear of being incapacitated....
Michael:	The fear is that I think I'm losing control...and yet once there is the freedom to cry, and the freedom to be *in it*, then it's clear that that's an incorrect [perception].

Since a man is often required to make the burial and memorial arrangements and to see that obligations and responsibilities to other people are met, Michael's reaction was not untypical. Often, a survivor fears that if he shows his sadness, there will be no end to it.

If you are among those who feel that you do not know how intense, lengthy, or deep your expression of grief may be, you may find yourself thinking that it would be impossible — or at least very difficult — for you to pull out of grief's deep pit to do all the things you need to do before or after the death. Being afraid of getting sucked down into a hollow of "no return" is not realistic. *Grief is not quicksand. Rather, it is a walk on rocky terrain that eventually smooths out and provides less challenge — both emotionally and physically.* So if you find yourself fearful of grieving, if you're imagining the worst or expecting some untenable transformation to take place within yourself, try putting those catastrophic thoughts in their proper perspective.

For example, you may think: *I will fall apart and won't be able to function if I start to show how I feel.* Replace such a thought with the more realistic: *I will let go for a time, release what I feel, and will be able to function better as a result of having vented the feelings that are an ever-present burden.*

You may think: *If I let myself grieve, then I will change permanently and won't ever be able to be myself again.* It's a fact that grief changes most survivors whether or not they vent their emotions and express their feelings. You can't keep change from happening after a loss; it is part of surviving a death. But you can take control over the *type* of change you experience. As you allow yourself to grieve, the changes that take place will be ones which allow you to go forward, to integrate loss, and to resolve the issues related to your loved one's death. Venting your responses can be like turning a searchlight on something moving in the shadows — which you imagine to be more enormous and menacing than it really is. Once the light is on, your caution seems to have been completely unnecessary.

As you *acknowledge and allow the total range of your emotions, you'll experience an additional feeling of release if you can communicate about your grief.* It may mean coming out of an envelope of silence to express your feelings.

Communicating About the Loss

A psychologist working with bereaved parents made this statement about the way some men work through a loss: "It depends on how strong the cultural impact is on the individual person. The more culturally traditional the person is, the more difficult it will be. When a man feels comfortable with crying from time to time, when he can talk about his pain without feeling a loss of face to his wife, close friends or a particular person, then he does okay. *When he bottles all that stuff up, it is so very difficult.*"

> We have noted that...silence is defensive, designed to protect men against being vulnerable to their own dependency needs. The silence proclaims the lie that men do not need others, and the lie undermines the mutual need that binds couples, families, friendships, and communities. It is true that silent men are also frightened, but that does not excuse the lie, the mistrust, or the damage caused by the self-protected silence, nor does it ease the pain inside men's hearts.
> (Stephen Shapiro, *Manhood*)

In a study conducted following the suicide of a child, the researchers reported that two-thirds of the fathers refused to be interviewed themselves, and 50 percent of them refused interviews that were to be held with their wives. When the wives said they were willing to participate, their husbands turned down the interview, stating that the wife could not endure it. It seems apparent that the husband had more fear of revelation than the wife.

A woman who survived the loss of a teenager expressed her view of the differing ways in which she and her husband grieved the loss of their son.

> There are very different feelings and attitudes that men and women have toward the grieving process. Because men are not able to say what they feel, it makes the grieving harder and makes the situation at home more difficult. Men don't reach out to find help and support. Women will read books on the mourning process or on

suicide, and can relay that information to the husband or male who will listen, but who won't actually read the material or find the material himself.

The reluctance to talk is not confined to any age group. In a study of college students who had lost a loved one, the researchers found the women students were more willing to talk and express feelings than were the men. One of the men who did participate in the discussion described his "male silence" following the death of his sister.

My family never spoke about the death. At 17 years of age when the death occurred, I had no idea about the loss. Maybe a little more openness on the part of my family would have helped. To this day, my father cannot be spoken to about the death of his oldest daughter. It is an unspoken rule.

(Quoted in La Grand, "Loss Reactions of College Students: A Descriptive Analysis," *Death Education*)

In interviews with men who had lost a parent, the majority had not discussed the loss with their surviving siblings. Every man who had not discussed his parent's death expressed relief at being able to recall memories and feelings during the interview process and expressed the wish that he had discussed his reaction to the loss earlier.

Being able to talk about the variety of emotions that the death of your loved one produces, especially guilt, anger, and fear, will lessen the probability that such emotions will be turned inward where they may produce debilitating conditions or, at the extreme, self-destructive behavior.

Finding the Language for Your Grief

At first, talking about your loved one's death will be very difficult. You may be able to talk about the *facts* of the death, but not the *emotional impact* it has had on you. For example, a survivor may communicate by saying something similar to: "My son died one day before his twelfth birthday," or "My wife had been going to the doctor for six months before they correctly diagnosed her condition. She'd had cancer all along." Or "When my dad knew he was sick, he asked me to come home, and I didn't go," or "My mother was on morphine before she died," or, "The car my fiance was riding in was small and provided no protection in the crash."

Each one of these statements relates a fact. In order to release grief-related emotions, it's important to get behind the *fact* to the *emotion* it produced. The survivor whose son died before his birthday would ask himself, "How did I feel about my son dying a day before his birthday? What special impact did that have?" Of course, a son dying one day before his birthday would tragically underscore the snuffing out of a young life, so the father might reply, "It makes me feel angry about how *unfair* my son's death was. It makes me feel powerless. I feel deserted by God."

The son whose dad asked him to come home but he didn't go might express his feelings as follows: "I feel guilty about that. I feel wrong and selfish. I wish I could do the whole thing over. I wish I could know dad forgave me for not coming to see him."

The man who said, "My mother was on morphine before she died," would need to ask himself how that made him feel. His answer might be, "I felt as if I were going to cry when I saw her in such pain. My stomach hurt. My throat closed up. I wanted to trade places with her so she could get some relief and I could suffer in her place."

If you find yourself talking about your loved one's death in a factual way, rather than in a way that conveys your emotions, you may remind yourself that you can get behind the reportorial part of the loss to the *core* of the loss by using a vocabulary which permits emotions: *I feel, I need, I wish, I miss,* rather than *I think.*

You may have the desire to talk about your feelings, but also have reservations about who makes a safe, supportive listener. The listener who will be the most helpful to you will be someone who is nonjudgmental, accepting, able to hear the bad as well as the good, and not afraid of anger.

The listener who is not helpful will:

- Say that talking doesn't do any good

- Counsel you not to be weak, or to express too much pain or sadness

- Urge you to think of others who are "worse off"

- See your expression of sadness, longing, or despair as un-manly, a waste of time, or an indication of impending col-lapse

- Urge you to focus on tomorrow and forget the past

Aiding Expression as a Caregiver

It is important for caregivers and those closest to the sur-vivor to be alert to a man's need to talk and to solicit his feelings. By speculating gently and kindly, a caregiver is sending the signal to the survivor that *communication is okay.* It is *acceptable,* even *desirable.*

Such a solicitation needs to be appropriate for the man's specific situation and personality type. For example, a discussion may be opened in one of the following ways:

- You must have lots of things that you are going over in your mind.

- What is giving you the most trouble now? What do you think about the most? Miss the most?

- Do you think talking about the way you feel would make someone else feel bad?

- Are you sleeping at night? Are certain thoughts keeping you awake?

- Are you having difficulty concentrating during the day? What happens at those times?

- What happened the day of the death? Do you want to talk about it?

- How would you describe your relationship with your oldest son? (Or father, lover, wife, and so on.)

The environment for such an exchange should be private — at home, in the car, on a walk, in a one-to-one talk after work, or in the office of a helping professional. There should be sensitivity to time and outside intrusion. It would not be wise, for example, to solicit someone's feelings and then "have to run" to another appointment, take care of an errand, or go home. Such behavior would seem uncaring, even rejecting, and it would intensify the survivor's tendency to retreat into silence. A person who cares for and about a man who has lost a loved one, will show a sincere willingness to listen and discuss, and to validate the person's death and the impact that person's dying has made on the survivor.

> I think the best thing that could have happened to me is to have had some understanding person who could know what I was going through listen to me, listen to the agony I was going through.
>
> *(Survivor of father loss)*

The majority of men who are survivors are masking or holding in *some* emotion most of the time, and, if given encouragement and unconditional acceptance, will be able to open up. A facilitator for a parents' grief group made this observation: "In our society men are taken seriously because they *don't* open up, because they *don't* talk about their feelings. Women aren't taken seriously because they *do* talk about their feelings."

At first, men will say they don't want to "dwell" on it. "We're not going to go on all night about this," they'll say. Men are expected to rise above the need for the expression of feelings. It's interesting that women talk about it, analyze it, discuss it, get it out, and that this same process is viewed by some men as *"dwelling on it."* Again, it is the portrayal of vulnerabilty and pain that is being resisted.

A forty-year-old Vietnam vet talked about the relief he experienced as a result of being expressive.

> Women have always been liberated in the important ways, in emotional ways. And men have never had that liberation *yet*. Men need to be more honest with their feelings and let them out.... Part of my growth has been *that*...to become more emotional, to let things out. I've learned a lot from women in that way. Believe me, I know how to act when I'm around a lot of stoic men. I just kind of play into their trip a little bit so they won't be uncomfortable, when actually I prefer to

be very tender and loving...and sensitive...and talk
about things, get things off my back right away.

As a man's feelings are liberated, as the stuff that makes his
nightmares is unbottled, such expression may permit the release
of his tears, which is still another vital channel for sadness, despair, and vulnerability. As Therese Rando stated in *Grief, Dying
and Death*, we need to "assist men in dealing with the socially
conditioned responses that block grief resolution. Give men permission to grieve and help them learn to cry."

Releasing Tears

For some reason, our society seems to have equated the control
of problems with the control of tears. It seems as if we believe a
person cannot be efficient or capable if he cries. For example, in
1972, Senator Muskie lost his bid for the presidential nomination
shortly after he cried in frustration over a vicious and inaccurate
news story about his wife.

These views about men's tears are now slowly changing.
There are even places, such as men's groups, where the environment not only permits male tears, but encourages them. Groups
such as these are not in abundance, but at least they do exist.
And that's a start in allowing men to express their deepest feelings — for we cry not only when we are sad, but also when we
feel despair, great happiness, exhaustion, extreme frustration, surprise, or a number of other conditions and emotions.

It's interesting to note that in a study of adult crying behavior, researcher William Frey reported that "male crying was 3
percent greater than that of women in an ambiguous causal category labeled 'sad thoughts.'" In discussing sadness with men
who are survivors, another ambiguous category appears, which
can be called "an underlying sense of tragedy." It is a kind of
grief that is linked to all other griefs, or is the product of all grief,
and it may or may not be associated with death.

There have been a few times in my life, years apart
usually, when I will spontaneously weep. I'm not
unhappy about anything and I'll be getting dressed to
go somewhere or there is something out of the blue.
There will be a commercial on the radio, or a car

drives by, or a girl is bouncing a ball down a sidewalk, and I just go to pieces and just blubber for a few minutes. It's not tied to anything, nothing conscious, just out of the blue. I've never linked this with my father's death. The tragic quality built into the universe just gets me for a moment. It's just so sad and I blubber about it and then I go back to what I'm doing. At a conscious level, I don't think about my father. It doesn't even cross my mind that it [the crying] has anything to do with him. It's like my system needed to do this, and something just set it off.

(35-year-old survivor of parental death)

Crying Is a Human Need

It is important to recognize that crying is a *human need*. People were given the ability to cry for a very real reason. Studies have shown that babies having an illness which makes them unable to generate tears also have an extremely low tolerance for emotionally stressful events.

Thomas Scheff, author of *Catharsis in Healing, Ritual and Drama*, calls tears a "necessary biological component." Crying helps relieve emotional stress. Holding back tears causes additional stress which may result in physical and psychological symptoms. In fact, some scientists believe that tears remove from the body toxic substances which are caused by stress. If emotional tension is not relieved, it can exacerbate existing conditions such as high blood pressure, gastric and duodenal ulcers, colitis, allergies, and cardiovascular diseases.

Thus, the male of the English-speaking world who is everywhere taught that "a little man" doesn't cry, having repeatedly been caused to repress his desire to weep until he has become incapable of weeping from his lacrimal glands, often begins, in later life, to weep through his skin or his gastrointestinal tract. It is now well established that in a large proportion of cases of atopic dermatitis, there is associated a strong but inhibited desire to weep.

(Ashley Montagu, *Touching*)

Just as a release of certain feelings can be feared as a forerunner of collapse, you may link crying with the fear of not being able to "get it together." Once I begin to cry, you may speculate, who knows what may happen? I may not be able to stop.

Prolonged, "unstoppable" crying is not something you need to worry about. In fact, in William Frey's study on adult crying behavior conducted with 45 men and 286 women, researchers found that the average length of a crying session was six minutes. What you may term a "break down" is, in actuality, only a brief respite from built-up emotional tension.

A father whose children died described his outbursts:

> Monotonous, isn't it: this man going on about how he cries all the time. Forgive him: he knows what he's doing, more or less, but it's still too early for him to have any real control over it....Burst into tears without warning this afternoon; lay on the floor in the empty house and howled. Couldn't understand what had provoked it — there's usually a trigger of some kind. Then realized: it's Friday afternoon, my internal clock still synchronized to them; it was precisely the time when I would have been driving across to Belgrave to pick them up for the weekend. And it came home to me then that this has been happening every Friday since they died.
>
> (John Tittensor, *Year One*)

In grief, your periods of crying may be very frequent, but you can be fairly certain that your crying will not continue uncontrollably for unreasonably long periods. For example, widowers often speak of "crying all day." What they actually do is cry for short periods of time on and off throughout the day or night. Perhaps because the widower is usually living alone, it is easier for him to "let go."

> I was a basket case for the first month. I would get up in the morning and cry. I would cry until I had no tears left.
>
> (*Widower surviving the loss of his wife of 35 years*)

Crying As a Signal

In addition to directly affecting your health, crying can be an important signal to other members of your family as well. It's a signal that says, "It's okay to grieve." It shows the other survivors that you share their sadness and loneliness, and that you loved the person who has died.

Dr. E. James Lieberman, Clinical Professor of Psychiatry at George Washington University School of Medicine writes, "Adults fear to let their children see them weep, and so the children think that crying, even over death, is immature, a loss of self-control, unmanly, soft, overemotional, indulgent. Organization man views grief as a threat to order, objectivity, intellect, and morale. The ability to face — and inflict — grief without flinching is an essential virtue of the effective soldier, whether in khaki or a gray flannel suit. The antigrief posture is the hallmark of strategic defence in the nuclear age."

But children are not comfortable with this "antigrief" posture. As pointed out in chapter 4, children and adolescents are very tuned in to their parents' behavior following a death, and they watch to see what course the parent takes.

> My dad felt like he had to support the whole family. I know he loved my brother, but I wanted him to be sad, to cry.
>
> *(Teenaged girl whose brother died of leukemia)*

It may be an enormous relief for a child to see tears. Tears can represent an important display of affection, as well as grief at the loss. The surviving child needs to know that the father loved.

Of course, it's certainly not true that tears are always a sign of love. In fact, there are people who can cry, quite convincingly, over someone they actually care very little about. The point here is that it is unnecessary for you to remain stoic, and doing so may even misrepresent your ability to be empathic, compassionate, and loving. Again, it is the willingness to be vulnerable to those emotions which strike closest to the human core that will ultimately help you work through grief.

Feeling Free To Cry

If you feel you are holding back tears that need to be shed, you can set up several situations for yourself in which you will be free to cry. Male survivors have sought and gained relief in several ways.

Ted was the caretaker for his friend Alan, who was terminally ill. Ted tells of how he stuffed down his feelings and kept himself from crying as he went through anticipatory grief.

> Before Alan died, I had two emotions. One was grief that he was going, and the other was pure anger that a 29-year-old kid had to die. There was a roller coaster of grief to extreme anger. At that point, I would feel tears coming and I would shut them down, think about something else.

As a survivor of Alan's death, Ted found that he benefitted from crying, that it provided him with a necessary catharsis. Because of this, he arranged his day so that during one part of it he could be alone to cry, and he allotted himself ample time to do it. Ted encouraged other men who are survivors to do the same.

> My advice would be to take some time for yourself every day, at least an hour. I'm getting up an hour earlier in the morning, and I sit out in the garden just to give myself time to center. And also to cry. I think it's very hard for men in our culture to cry, and to give yourself the freedom to do that. To give yourself the freedom to actively grieve. And if that means sobbing for ten minutes, that's okay.

A father whose three-year-old son died in an accident, told of walking on an isolated path in the woods every day, crying, freely calling for his child, yelling if he wanted to. Then the father would return, "temporarily drained and tired, but *relieved*. The pressure was off me for a while."

Another father who was surviving the loss of a child said he felt that by "trying to be strong for my wife I was standing in my own way. I was my own obstacle to resolving my loss. When I recognized this and held my wife and cried with her, I found that we both felt more connected and closer in our grief. When we expressed it together, the world didn't come to an end. Nobody fell apart."

Eliciting Tears

For some men, crying may not seem possible. That is, for them it may not simply be a matter of allowing and releasing tears that are already there. Some survivors report that they feel the need for emotional release through crying, but the tears won't come. These are the men who say, "I want to open up," or "I feel the need to let out my feelings, but I don't know how," or "I don't know where to start."

Such a survivor may say that his situation is making him feel:

- Exhausted

- On guard

- Stifled

- Constricted

- Frustrated

- Bottled up

- Angry

He may also have a worrisome physical condition such as a sore back, rapid heartbeat, constriction in his throat, or shaking hands.

If you identify with these reactions and you feel the need to let out your grief-related emotions, try setting up a situation for yourself which will produce the maximum opportunity for you to release your feelings. First, you need to arrange for time alone.

Visiting your private place. You may find it helpful to select a private place in your house (or elsewhere) where you can go to grieve. For some people it is sitting at a desk in a den, at a dresser in a bedroom, or in a secluded area in the garden. For others, it may be on a sofa in a basement away from family activities, in a friend's studio, in a church sanctuary, or even at the gravesite in the cemetery. Wherever you choose, it needs to be a place where you feel comfortable, one which allows you the space and solitude necessary for experiencing and expressing emotions. It's especially important for you not to be anxious or fearful of interruption. In the place you choose you may keep (or take with you) a photograph, memento, letter, possession, or even an article of clothing that reminds you of your loved one. Some survivors refer to this place as their personal "shrine" to the person who died.

When you are there you may focus your thoughts on:

- How you met your loved one (or the day your child was born, or your earliest memory of your loved one).

- The things that the two of you enjoyed doing together.

- The one thing you'll miss most.

- Your loved one's best qualities.

- The most important or memorable thing your loved one said to you.

- The special way your loved one looked.

- The expression he or she had at times of great happiness.

- How he or she looked when performing an ordinary daily task.

- The way your loved one looked when he or she was eager to tell you something.

- The way he or she looked when expressing love.

Review the daily tasks in which you and your loved one interacted, the habits the two of you had, or some small moment you shared on a regular basis, such as your wife's good-bye in the morning, your young son's bedtime routine and story, your lover's kiss upon waking, your dad's daily telephone call.

You may go to this private place often at first. You may even like the idea of scheduling a specific time period for a "visit." When you're there, let the feelings that you've been holding inside rise to the surface. Whatever rises, accept it. You may feel only a deep despair and loneliness tugging at you slowly and steadily like a sorrowful undercurrent. You may feel angry or frightened. You may feel abandoned, confused, and childlike. You may simply wish to yearn aloud. One survivor told of sitting in his bedroom, holding his wife's robe in his arms, clutching it to his chest, and crying, "Oh, I miss you, I miss you so," over and over again.

As you allow your own deep feelings to surface, you may find that your eyes grow damp or you may begin to cry. You may even find yourself sobbing. One bereaved father described making a sound he had never heard before, one which frightened him and made him question his own sanity. If you find yourself making a moan, a shout, or a choking sound, it's perfectly acceptable for you to do so and you shouldn't be alarmed or ashamed. Remember, any such expression that is within you is *real* and you should respect it and allow it to occur. There is nothing about your expression of emotion that you need to explain to yourself or to anyone else. It is simply you doing what you need to do. A fifty-two-year-old painter whose son died of cancer told of rocking back and forth, holding a pillow like a child, even curling up on the floor at times.

Whatever feelings you express or experience will pass after awhile. When such expressions are especially powerful or prolonged, they are physically tiring and, as one bereaved brother said, "just make a person go numb, eventually." But it's important to recognize that in the overall course of your loss these expressions allow you to lighten your burden of grief.

Putting your thoughts and feelings into words. Sometimes it helps to say things to your loved one. You may have feelings that you never fully expressed when your loved one was alive. Or, as one young survivor said of losing his mother, "I never got to say good-bye to her. I'd give anything if I could have two minutes to say good-bye." Alone, in your private place, you may feel free to say anything you like. You may take care of any "unfinished business" which has been occupying your thoughts.

There are several ways you may go about doing this. For example, you may visualize your loved one sitting in front of you in an empty chair. Or you may close your eyes and develop an image of your loved one in any setting you desire. Or you may look at a recent photograph of your loved one and focus your attention on it rather intently for a period of time.

After you have established a feeling of closeness, begin to think about what you'd like to say to your loved one that you did not have a chance to say when he or she was living. Think of all the emotions, thoughts and concerns you need to put into words. They may include any of the following:

- Feelings of gratitude, appreciation, or love

- Feelings of loss or abandonment

- Feelings about the last days of your loved one's life

- Feelings about your loved one's pain

- Things from the past that you regret or feel guilty about

- Concerns for your loved one's current state — his or her life after death

- Fears about your life without your loved one's presence

- Concerns about how your loved one would react to choices you are making now or might make later on

- Things you want your loved one to know about your current grief, about how you are being affected by the loss

- Ways you would like your loved ones' support — even now, after death

You may want to try to say some of these things aloud. The sound of your own voice may help in the catharsis. Don't attempt to make your voice sound the way you imagine it should sound. For example, don't try to flatten out emotion that is present in your voice, and don't think that you need to put into your voice any emotion that you don't feel. Just let your voice do what it wants to do.

Some survivors have even described feeling the need for a response from their loved one. If you feel this way, you may imagine how your loved one would comment on what you are saying. Then you can say that answer aloud. If talking aloud seems too strange to you, whisper what you want to say or say it subvocally; that is, *imagine* yourself saying the words. You can gain relief by just allowing the words to form in your mind and experiencing them as a message or statement to your loved one. Again, don't worry if having this sort of conversation seems unusual or childish. It is neither. It is simply another way of working through some of the unfinished aspects of your loss.

The Major Ways To Experience Relief

Up to this point we have discussed three ways to vent your grief and release tears. They are:

1. By crying with other family members and not being fearful about everything going to pieces.

2. By setting aside or "building in" extra time before the day begins during which you can give yourself permission to be alone and feel your deepest feelings.

3. By setting up a place of memorial to your loved one, a private place where the whole range of your emotions (even the wildest outbursts of grief) can be unleashed.

Still another important channel can be used for the relief and release of your grief: you may join a group which will offer emotional support — such as one exclusively for widowers, veterans, cancer survivors, bereaved parents, or AIDS survivors.

This last recommendation is an extremely important one. Support groups have been, and will increasingly continue to be places of transition for a man who is surviving a death. They are safe environments in which a man can leave behind more restrictive traditional behavior and allow himself to deal with his innermost painful feelings. The next chapter takes a look at overcoming the perceived risks in order to benefit from the release that is inherent in joining a group.

9

Sharing Grief on Common Ground

*In working with grief, a person has the opportunity
to uncover a lot of wonderful things about the self.
He has the opportunity to peel away a lot of
superficial layers and to re-examine his life, to
develop compassion for other people in his life, to
have a deeper sense of purpose.*
(GROUP FACILITATOR)

Because men are less accustomed to talking about emotional
issues, they're more likely than women survivors to be apprehen-
sive about attending a support group. It's certainly true that
while sharing grief with other survivors can be enormously beneficial, it can also be initially frightening.

When a man does attend a survivor group, he will usually
exhibit the characteristics of one or more of the following general
types of participants:

- The Open Participant

- The Observer

- The Consultant

- The Efficient Griever

- The Companion

- The Augmenter

Let's look at how each type of participant reacts within the group experience.

The Open Participant

This survivor is open to the group experience. He attends with a receptive attitude. He expects, appreciates, and responds to support and fellowship.

> Going to Hospice was a really good thing for me. I was able to talk, and the other participants were able to talk, and I was able to sort of let things out a little bit. The woman at Hospice told me, "We have volunteer counselors who conduct sessions, and if you'd like to do it and go through this whole process, why don't you do it?" It was for a ten-week period. The group had been formed specifically for people who had lost a parent. I was the only man. A woman in the group was very inspiring to me, although I didn't do the things she did. She did some art work, wrote some poems, put together some journals that she shared with us. It was good to see what she was doing. She was very expressive about how the death of her mother had really affected her. She was very disturbed by the death. I don't know if she was more disturbed than I was, but she was more expressive about it. I would come to every meeting just because of the kinds of things that all of us would talk about. It was really valuable in that way.
>
> *(49-year-old survivor of father's death)*

The participant who attends a group with a genuine desire to process his experience and to benefit from support will usually talk when it is his turn, tell his story, respond to the comments and experiences of others when it is appropriate, and establish some bonds within the group, even though they may be temporary.

The Observer

This survivor goes to the group to watch. He appears to maintain an emotional distance from those seeking release and support. In general, he is there to test the water, check out what's happening, and see if the territory is safe. He may remain quiet throughout the entire session.

The Consultant

The consultant stays in control and is analytical in regard to other survivors' situations and needs. He isn't self-revealing, but is attentive to others as they speak and he offers his solutions to their problems. As one counselor put it, "Then there is the man who comes, is stoic, and tells other people what they should do."

The Efficient Griever

This is the survivor whose mode of operation is "Let's get this over with." He comes into the group and says, "Here's the problem. Now fix it." He zeroes right in on what he wants to have solved, and he doesn't want to be delayed or diverted. Something isn't working and it's the group's job to get it running again. If the group doesn't respond with rapid, concrete "solutions," he loses interest and thinks he's wasting his time.

The Companion

This man attends the group "for his wife's sake." As the companion, he goes along to be supportive. He doesn't go to deal with his own grief. Even though grief may be recognized and discussed by all the other people in the group, he will act as if it has nothing to do with him personally.

The Augmenter

He accompanies his wife, or friend, or brother and adds to or expands upon what the other survivor is saying. He isn't the main communicator regarding their joint loss, but he will contribute to or correct the story told by his companion. He often fastens on details and speaks in order to straighten them out for the listener, making sure the picture is completely accurate in regard to facts.

Even though a survivor may fit very succinctly into one of the last five categories, it doesn't mean he will not benefit from the group experience. Usually, the man who continues to attend a support group will become increasingly open to the experience of processing his grief. For example, though he may start out as a Companion or an Observer, he may become more like an Open Participant after listening to others discuss their situations and grief-related concerns and feelings. Eventually, he will be able to open up, talk, and experience some benefit from release.

Benefits of Joining a Support Group

As participants discuss their reactions and responses to the death of a loved one, as they tell their own stories and explore their own immediate personal situations and concerns, the links in the circle of the grief group will strengthen, and the benefits of the individual survivor will increase.

Let's look now at four specific ways you can benefit from being in a group.

1. You can establish a connection with others who have experienced the same type of loss and who may be grappling with the same types of reactions, such as anger at the medical community, powerlessness, guilt for not showing "enough love" to the one who died, or fear of living alone or of being an inadequate single parent. You'll meet other survivors who may also fear being unable to cope with their new identity, or to understand *where* they go from *here*.

2. Grief for anyone is isolating. As soon as the death of your loved one occurs, you're likely to feel distanced from the real world, set apart from others, or even *undesirable* because you have been touched by death. In a group, that sense of being distanced melts away. You can emerge from the extremely isolating state of grief to a state of acceptance by others. This is particularly true if you are suffering from the stigma which accompanies a death resulting from suicide, homicide, or AIDS.

3. If you become a group member who fully participates, who really listens, who helps, and who calls to offer support to another member, you'll experience the beneficial effects of providing sincere and concerned attention for others who suffer. *Helping others gives you strength, renewed confidence, and purpose.* It also helps you to make some sense of things during a very confused time. Each time you accomplish an act of assistance and compassion,

you're utilizing one of the most important and valuable instincts of humankind, which is to lessen the suffering of others.

4. Participation in the group will provide you with a definite, reliable activity you can depend on to contribute continuity, predictability, and security to your life during a time of emotional turmoil and transition.

Other group members and facilitators usually realize that it takes courage for anyone to come to a group and that doing so may be a particularly alien act for a man, since men are generally less familiar than women are with sharing emotional issues among themselves. But if you genuinely seek relief and release, you'll take the necessary step to join a group and then find an acceptable way to get your needs met within the group's format.

Locating a Group

You can find a grief group by calling the nearest Hospice, pastoral care office at the hospital or church offices, or by reading notices in the local papers which announce the meetings of local support groups. Groups for specific types of loss can be located by contacting organizations which address those losses, such as SIDS (Sudden Infant Death Syndrome), Compassionate Friends (bereaved parents), POMC (Parents of Murdered Children and Other Survivors of Homicide Victims), or AIDS projects.

Up to this point, the discussion has focused on grief groups which have participants of both sexes. Although the mixed group is the most prevalent type, in some areas all-male groups are available. This type of group has a stronger appeal for many men; that is, men in an all-male group will usually prefer the men's group to a mixed group, if given a choice.

The All-Male Grief Group

There is nothing complicated about the men's support group that I belong to, nothing wildly exceptional about the men in it, except, perhaps, that they are willing to meet in this way at all. Nevertheless, the

evenings we spend together produce in me a feeling
so deep it is hard to speak of. After a couple of
meetings, I felt I had six new friends — and male
friends are not easy to come by in this world — whom
I could turn to in any circumstances. I had a place
where I could go and discuss whatever was
happening to me, however difficult, shameful, or
embarrassing. I felt I had a place where I was being
entirely who I was, where other men were being who
they were, and that being ourselves gave us a kind of
power that no one of us could have had himself.

(David Guy, *The Independent,*
North Carolina)

Generally, an all-male group provides an even more comfortable
common ground on which to share grief. In such a gathering,
"we're all in this thing together" is the prevailing attitude. A
counselor/facilitator for an exclusively male group told how men
who had been in both types of groups compared the two. "They
talked about the difference between being in the mixed group
and being in the men's group. They said that the men's group
offered a different kind of support. Nobody discounted what had
happened in the mixed groups, but it was like something was
missing."

Discussions in the men's group had a different emphasis on
certain issues, sex being one of the most prominent. The men's
group facilitator stated, "The men can discuss issues of sexuality
and relationships with women in a different way. There's just
more of a biological understanding, first of all, but also there's
understanding in terms of our socialization, what we're up
against as men in this culture, and some of the problems we may
be facing. There's a sense of brotherhood. There's something
about being with a man that's almost a tribal thing, the going
back. Men together support each other in being men. I think part
of that seems to be almost genetic, like there's a genetic memory
or something. Women who are together feel that too. They feel
that there's a special kind of energy."

Another facilitator reported, "In terms of talking about sexuality and talking about women, men felt much more comfortable
talking about that in the men's group. Some of them said they
never would have brought up certain subjects in a mixed group,

more as a sign of respect to the women than a sign of discomfort." He further pointed out, "Just in the course of men getting together to talk about anything, sex may come up as a part of life. It's an important part of life for a lot of people. It's interwoven, the loss and the sexuality."

Sexual Issues

Male survivors are concerned with varying sexual issues. Fathers who survive the loss of a child may find themselves feeling "wrong" about expecting to have a normally active sexual relationship after the death of the child. For example, in the first few weeks following the death, the husband may want to continue with the same kind and frequency of sexual intimacy that the couple had before the death of the child, but his wife may view it as inappropriate. On the other hand, his wife may be sexually inclined while he is not. Either situation can produce discomfort or a feeling of rejection on the part of one partner. Among widowers, the prominent sexual issues are sexual loneliness and longing, and fear of impotency or inadequacy. The longer and more monogamous a man's marriage was, the more intense his concern is likely to be. A widower may feel that he needs to prove to himself that he is "okay" (still able to be sexually intimate) within the first few months following the loss. On the other hand, he may need physical comforting, tenderness and nurturance, rather than sex, but he may believe that it is only through sex he can get the affection and attention he desires.

Fear of Losing Control

In addition to sexual concerns, one of the prominent issues in the men's group is losing control. A men's group facilitator described it this way: "Men are concerned about losing control, being overwhelmed by grief feelings, and being unable to function on the job. There is the fear of not being able to take care of business. For men that is *much* stronger. Generally, men identify more with their minds, with their intellects...and it's more a part of their identity in a lot of ways. So when something threatens *that*, it's more scary. Because what they identify with the most is their cognitive skill. And sometimes it just doesn't function. Quite a few men were talking about that. They started forgetting things, or things weren't like they used to be in terms of clarity of thought."

Permission to Cry

In a men's group, being given permission to cry is especially freeing. Even though participants are given this permission (either orally or by example) in a mixed group, among men this acceptance is more uninhibiting. The participant learns that he does not need to refrain from talking about something which is painful for fear he will cry.

Gary was a veteran who had not been able to cry, regardless of losing his closest lifelong friend. He didn't cry when his friend was killed in Vietnam nor when his own mother died. "Again, I couldn't cry, couldn't cry. Didn't have any feeling..."

Gary "found" his feeling when he attended a veteran's support group. This was an important turning point for him. When asked what advice he would give to another vet who was having the same difficulties, he offered this recommendation:

I would tell that person [a survivor who inhibits his grief] and I've *told* that person before — because I've *known* that person — when it gets too bad and when you're ready, get help at one of these support groups. I noticed relief after the very first session. I talked about my partner [best friend] dying and it was the first time I had talked about it and it was also the first time I was able to cry. Now I can be off by myself sometimes, think about it, and I'll start to cry, but *I had never been able to cry before* that day.

When he was asked about how his crying began, about how a grieving man undergoes change within an accepting group of men, Gary told of the typical macho attitude, and how it dissolves when a man's peers show their acceptance of tears and when they create a permissive atmosphere which encourages the expression of feelings.

We have two new members in the vets' group. Those two new people. They were like me a couple of years ago. They drove up, smoking cigarettes and gritting their teeth. We were talking in the group about the format [that first night], how we go about the group and everything, and one of the old timers [previous group members] mentioned, "Hey, if you're talking and you feel like crying, go for it, man. I have. This is the place you can come and cry and let it out." And then those two new guys look at him and take it in. It's not like, "Oh, I ain't going to cry." It's like they take it in and listen to it. Now, I don't see embarrassment when someone cries and I don't think he feels embarrassment once he cries and sees the initial positive response. It may be just someone commenting, "Hey, it's all right man." Or just sitting quietly and letting it run its course.

One time I was talking about my friend who died and I could hardly talk, like I wanted to cry and I had to stop for a minute. The guy across from me, showing his compassion, said, "Hey, I hear you man. It's like your throat really gets tight and you can't even talk..." He didn't have to come up and put his arm around me, but he *showed* me and that was his way. It was the same as him coming over and comforting me.

A facilitator described how crying was accepted within his all-male group:

There was real respect for the men in that way. There was an okay-ness about having their own feelings and experiencing them in a group-supported way. This seems to be one of the major ways in which men's and women's groups differ. Women would have more of a tendency to take care of and to want to comfort and support, which is real valuable at times. But [with] men it's almost as if they're saying, "I know you have the strength and I'm there for you." There was respect for each other's strength.

An entirely different set of circumstances usually prevails when survivors are in public or when others visit their homes. In fact, it is safe to say that at one time or another every male who loses a loved one experiences the awkwardness, resentment, or feeling of isolation that comes when friends approach him and don't talk about the death, ignore the fact that it occurred, or tell him to cheer up because he has to go on with his life. The survivor may begin to question the value of his friends and colleagues at such times. If their interactions are superficial, if his friends do not hear, listen, watch or care, the male survivor will be more likely to avoid any attempt at meaningful interactions. Instead, he'll save his "real life" for those who can solicit his heartfelt feelings and listen to his honest responses.

In summary, three of the key differences between women's and men's groups are that in all-male groups the participants are more likely to (1) discuss issues regarding the fear of loss of control, (2) discuss sexual concerns, and (3) release feelings in an environment that allows tears among men.

> I would say that in our society men are much more
> isolated from each other than women are. Men aren't
> really taught to relate with their feelings and their
> vulnerabilites and emotions. Women are given the okay
> to do that more, and that's what you need, really, to
> establish close relationships, so men tend to look
> toward women to do that. They're taught "we can do
> that with women, but not with men." That's why
> men's groups are so important. They educate men.
> They can be nurturing with each other and not have to
> just look toward women for emotional nurturing.
> There's something about men being together that can
> be equally nourishing, although in a different way.
> *(Men's group facilitator)*

Forming an All-Male Group

Now that the positive effects of men's groups have been explored, it may be helpful to look at the way in which a men's group can come into existence. The procedures presented here for forming, facilitating, and participating in an all-male group, are offered for the benefit of the many men who do not have access to such a group. As these guidelines are explored, the benefits of establishing such a grief group will be further evident.

Facilitator. The facilitator should be someone who has experienced the loss of his or her loved one at least a year prior to assuming a leadership role. Ideally, he should also be a lay counselor or a professional counselor, psychologist, or other professional in the helping field who has had some previous experience in facilitating a group. If the survivor has no previous experience, he should recruit an experienced person to serve as co-facilitator.

Soliciting members. There are several ways to solicit participants for such a group.

- Letters may be sent out to men who have already been identified as survivors by grief organizations. They may have been in some type of support program as they went through the process of terminal illness with a child or spouse, or they may have attended a mixed grief group one or two times, and then stopped coming.

- Fliers can be distributed at mental health conferences, meetings, classes, or seminars so that people in the helping professions can pass the information on to individuals as well as survivors' groups.

- Fliers can be posted on bulletin boards in churches, businesses, men's centers, libraries, hospitals, and sent directly to pastoral care and mental health workers.

- Notices can be placed in the newsletters of local grief organizations (or of the local chapters of national organizations).

The flier, notice, or letter should include the following information for prospective participants.

1. A statement explaining that the group is for men who have lost a loved one (a spouse, parent, child, friend, sibling or lover).

2. The name of the organizer or facilitator and a short description of that person's credentials or experience, possibly including a brief mention of his personal loss. (For example, "Steve Davidson, a high school teacher and twenty-year resident of Columbus, is a survivor of spousal loss.")

3. The location of the group's meeting place and directions for getting there.

4. The day of the week and the date of the first meeting.

5. The starting and finishing time of the meetings.

6. An announcement of any special aspect of the event (presentation of a film, speaker, or panel discussion, availability of coffee and dessert, wine and cheese and so on.)

7. A statement explaining that there is no fee for attending the group.

Duration and size. Generally, a successful group should meet over an eight to ten week period and be composed of between eight and fifteen participants. If the group exceeds fifteen men, there will not be adequate time for everyone to have an opportunity to share and participate in discussions. If there are fewer than eight, the group can still be very worthwhile, but in the smaller group the energy level will suffer if several participants happen to be absent at the same time.

Basic Orientation, Procedures, and Guidelines

The way in which the group functions is important. Too much or too little structure impedes the group's value. Let's examine how the group's aims are presented to the participants (*orientation*), what the group will do (*procedures* and *activities*), and how the group will go about maintaining contacts and meeting individual needs (*special considerations* and *guidelines*).

Orientation

The most immediate and important task is to establish trust in regard to expressing emotions and talking about feelings. The facilitator will find it beneficial to start by talking about the cultural restrictions which can influence and limit a man's grieving process. As a counselor-facilitator advised, "Be sure to emphasize that our culture doesn't generally permit men to cry. In the first and second session, we talked about the difficulty men have in our culture in getting in touch with their emotions. We talked about feeling vulnerable."

In the first session, the facilitator can explain that survivors' groups usually begin by sharing experiences. To relieve any possible anxiety the members may have, the facilitator may explain that he will start the sharing by telling something about his own loss. Then he will invite others to do the same. He should emphasize that each person can say as little or as much as he likes. If a participant doesn't wish to say anything at all, that is perfectly acceptable.

Procedures

The facilitator's role is to give each person a chance to speak and, at the same time, to move the sharing period along so that the meeting does not run overtime. Each person needs to have an opportunity to talk, but if any survivor wishes to listen without sharing, his preference should be respected.

The facilitator may also point out that actively listening to what others say is an essential part of belonging to the group. But it is not permissible to listen only for the purpose of volunteering similar information about one's self. For example, sometimes a survivor will automatically use another's experience as a springboard to relay his own experience. He may say, "Oh yes, when that happened to me...." It is helpful to have a rule that no one interrupts while the speaker is talking.

A counselor emphasized, "You don't need a lot of special techniques to elicit feeling. Everyone's feeling so much that just having a place for the men to empty is enough."

Balancing grief work and education. The group sessions can be balanced between actual grief work and education about the grieving process. Part of the time the participants can process their grief, and the other part of the time can be spent in getting new information, insights, and perceptions about grief-related issues. Such learning experiences can be provided by a visiting counselor, psychologist, pastoral care worker, grief consultant, or author in the field of grief who comes in to discuss an issue of particular interest to the group. The most effective topics for visitors to cover are those in which members have shown interest at previous meetings.

When the actual processing of grief is taking place, it is important not to interject information which will take the griever from the emotional process to a thinking and analytical process. One process should be allowed to come to a natural end before the other one begins.

As the sharing process takes place, it's important to have faith in it, to believe that it will have its own unique (and invisible) healing properties. *What may appear to be simply a circle of people sharing painful thoughts, feelings, and circumstances over and over again, is in actuality a group of individuals who are taking huge steps toward the genuine resolution of a loved one's death.*

Allow coasting. Sometimes men may come to the group and talk about something other than their losses. The subject may be a news event, a movie, baseball, the navy, business trends, cars, and so on. When this happens, it doesn't do any harm for such a conversation to continue. It may be that the participants are seeking a relief from the draining process of grief and are feeling the need to socialize for a while. Also, such an interval may be necessary to reestablish a feeling of trust, to infuse energy into the group, or to gear up for what they sense may lie ahead. When the conversation begins to slacken, the facilitator can solicit the sharing of grief-related issues, ask how the week has gone, and assist in the transition from socializing to processing.

Activities

Sharing materials. In general, people who are grieving are very anxious to share encouraging and supportive information and materials with others. There is a genuine desire to help the other griever, to alleviate pain whenever possible.

The male survivor can be encouraged to bring in something he's written that he would like to share. It could be a simple note, a letter, song, poem, or a description of his loved one. After he's shared it, others may want to chime in, expanding on the same theme, offering their own expressions or responses.

Each survivor can bring in a picture of the person whose death he is grieving and the men can share their pictures by passing them around, telling something about their loved one, and the context in which each picture was taken. The pictures can serve as a catalyst for reviewing the facets of the relationship that the survivor misses the most.

A member may want to share a book he's recently read and found to be particularly helpful. The facilitator of one men's group recalled, "There was one voracious reader who wanted to read everything about grief that had ever been written. At one point he bought each of the other members a copy of a book that he found to be helpful."

A reading list of books which deal most effectively with various types of issues or losses can be distributed to members. During one meeting, the facilitator may take a few minutes to summarize several of the books on the list and a display table can be set up so the participants can look through the available grief-related literature before and after the meeting.

Art for grief's sake. After the group has been together long enough to have achieved a comfortable familiarity, any one of a number of several art activities may be used. The participants can be invited to (1) draw what your grief looks like, (2) draw the feeling that is the most dominant and recurring (What color is it? How big is it?), (3) draw what you've been thinking about the most often during the past week, (4) draw how grief makes you look on the inside, or (5) draw a picture that shows your progress through grief.

After his picture is drawn, each survivor can show his drawing and talk about what he sees in it and what kind of response it provokes. Other members of the group may comment on the way in which they relate to the picture, the use of color, and so on.

Before beginning any one of these exercises (not more than one should be done in any single meeting), it is crucial for the participants to understand that their level of artistic skill is completely unimportant. The facilitator should emphasize that what is important is getting down what something feels like — what is inside the survivor's heart and in his mind.

Special Considerations and Guidelines

A number of special guidelines will increase the success of the group experience.

1. Guests should not be permitted to come into the session and watch. If a survivor who is looking for a group wants to visit and see what the group offers and the group is still in its first few meetings, it would be acceptable for him to come as a potential participant. It is not, however, appropriate for a survivor's friend or relative to attend when he has not actually been personally affected by the death and is not going to participate on equal terms with other survivors. Such a visitor would be invading the privacy of those who have a real purpose in their gathering.

2. Members should feel free to suggest topics or speakers for upcoming meetings.

3. A meeting should be scheduled before each major holiday or as close to the holiday as possible. Thanksgiving, Christmas, Hanukkah, or Easter may be very difficult times for survivors.

4. The death date and birthday of each survivor's loved one should be recorded. That member should be called on each of those dates by the facilitator and one or two other group members. Both are critical times for the survivor and he will need support.

5. Members should be invited to exchange telephone numbers if they're interested in doing so. If all the members of the group agree that they wish to exhange, the facilitator can prepare a master list of telephone numbers and distribute it during a meeting.

6. After the group has been together for enough time to have become familiar with one another's circumstances, a group activity may be planned. A baseball game, a dinner out, a concert, bowling, a play, a hike, camping, tennis, or a barbecue can provide a relaxed and revitalizing intermission away from the usual grief-focused activities.

Socializing outside the group. One of the bonuses of belonging to a group is the bond that is established among members. For example, two or three survivors may enjoy getting together on a regular basis for coffee, lunch, dinner or a movie. Men who have experienced this kind of companionship emphasize how rewarding it is to meet other men outside the context of business or some kind of competitive situation. "Instead we met, *just as we were*," a forty-two-year-old widower reported. "It was for the purpose of sharing what we were doing, listening to one another, and enjoying a few meaningful hours of companionship."

Men who have formed such bonds emphasize how important it is to have another man to count on, not merely to come through in a tight spot, but to understand who they are, what they think, what they feel, what their concerns, fears, hopes and dreams are — and, most importantly, to really care.

10

Writing the Way Through Grief

I absolutely think my writing saved my life when I was in Vietnam, because it was an outlet for my emotions. You had these moments of intense illumination brought on by many different stimuli. That's why in a lot of my writing there's a lot of darkness and a lot of experiences that come out that deal with tragedy, intense tragedy. I just started writing. There was something inside of me. I almost feel that it was a guardian angel...or a guide...or something, that was saying, "Get out." "Get out." "Get these things out." And I didn't know how to get these things out. I wasn't really getting the satisfaction from my friends that I really needed because they were turning to other things, to drugs, to prostitution, to violence....

(40-YEAR-OLD MEDIC)

Writing can be of tremendous help to you in the course of processing the various emotions, reactions, and conditions which are the direct result of your loss. If you decide to try working through some of your grief in this way, begin by telling yourself that any writing you are going to do will be done for yourself alone. You will be putting your words on paper for the purpose of freely exploring the core of your grief and allowing a fuller expression of your feelings.

Of course, how you choose to regard your writing — as private or not-so-private — will be your personal decision. There is no rule that says you can't tell others about it. In fact, some survivors write out their expressions of grief, and later decide to share them in a supportive environment, such as with a loved one or in a grief group. But, at the beginning, for the purpose of feeling free about what you are going to do it's necessary to give yourself permission to write with the intention that you alone will be the reader. No one else needs to know about, or read, what you write.

The Purposes and Benefits of Writing

In dealing with the many painful effects of losing your wife, parent, child, sibling, lover, or friend, writing can be of help in specific ways. For example, written expression can make it possible for you to:

- Confront and vent

- Yearn

- Connect or atone

- Explore

- Keep a thorough emotional and mental account of your grief

- "Keep" your loved one, or preserve a scene or an event

- Memorialize or create

- "Build" something

To Confront and Vent

Two of the most valuable purposes of grief-related writing are to confront and vent. In this kind of writing, you're able to give expression to a feeling (or feelings) that you cannot act out, find too confusing to explain, or too painful to talk about. To make such an exercise successful, you must first abandon self-censorship and have complete respect for your impulses. Second, you may need to prod yourself to follow your impulses, directly and honestly: *What am I feeling? What's getting me down? Are some thoughts more dominant than others? Which are they?*

Often, for many survivors the most prominent and disturbing feelings that they need to confront and vent are guilt and anger. Because there are both positive and negative aspects to any normal relationship, almost every survivor will have some feelings of guilt in regard to his interaction with his loved one. For example, many survivors view a loved one's death as having been preventable. The survivor takes responsibility for the loss, thinking that he has caused or contributed to the death.

If you have such a feeling, you may find it extremely difficult to deal with. Death often makes a survivor feel abandoned and powerless, which, in turn, causes him to feel angry. And anger, like guilt, is also difficult for him to dispel. Because being outwardly angry over an extended period of time is not permissible or possible in a normal social environment, the survivor will often deal with anger by exhibiting it partially or inhibiting it entirely. But *it won't go away* until he has vented it or directed it in some way. In fact, if it isn't released, anger will manifest itself in some other way, such as in physiological symptoms — heart palpitations, gastrointestinal disorders, exhaustion, nervousness, or insomnia. You may find that you have some degree of anger toward yourself, toward God, toward the unfairness of the world, toward your loved one who died, or something or someone else, depending upon your perceptions and tendencies and the specific situation in which you now find yourself.

If you expel anger on paper, you may actually unleash a whole gamut of other feelings as well, because anger seldom seethes all by itself; it is usually accompanied by other emotions. As you begin such an exercise, you may want to pose these questions to yourself: *What makes me feel the most anger? Why? What did the object of my anger do or not do? What do I think should have been done instead? How does anger make my body feel?* (This same pattern of questioning can also be used to unleash guilt.)

To vent such feelings as sadness, despair, and loneliness, you may answer these questions in writing: *When do I feel sadness (or another specific emotion) the most? What brings it on? What are all the things that make me sad now? What sadnesses did I have in the past which still cause me sorrow when I think of them? What color is sadness? How does it make my body feel?*

As you attempt to confront and vent each dominant grief-related feeling, *let it have it's way.* Every one of your feelings that seems to have no bounds, that does not diminish — every voice in your head that will not stop — can all be released harmlessly and productively on paper. This is one of the simplest channels you can use to help yourself through the grieving process.

To Connect or Atone

In this type of writing, you compose a letter to your loved one, telling him or her everything that you feel still needs to be said. Your letter serves as a safe place for finishing unfinished business. It allows you to say, "These are the things I want you to know now," or "These are the ways our relationship could have been better if I had known *then* what I know *now.* These are the things I could have done differently." You may reveal secrets: "Here's something I never told you." You may express for-giveness, or ask for forgiveness: "Please forgive me for being jealous, or for not being helpful enough, or being unfaithful, or not listening to you when you asked me to." The letter may also serve as your farewell, an in-depth, thorough good-bye to your loved one. In such a letter, you can relate what you and others will miss most, what you will always remember with fondness, what the relationship gave you, and how your life will be influ-enced by having known and loved that person. When a consid-erable period of time has passed after the death and you have worked through much of your grief, you may "ask" permission to start a new life, to work toward new goals, to invest in another relationship, or to focus on new ideas or activities.

To Yearn

Yearning isn't often discussed by survivors, yet it's a strong component of any grieving process because it's an instinctive re-sponse to a loved one's permanent absence. An Australian father who survived the death of his two children discussed his own grieving and longing in one of many journal entries:

Had to go for a walk in the bush this afternoon.
Knowing I would get upset and cry, but needing the
outlet. Stood there in the silence calling their names,
calling them back. From time to time a sound would
catch at me and I would stand, straining in the
direction it had come from; almost feeling that
if I listened hard enough I would hear them coming
through the bush and all would be restored.

(John Tittensor, *Year One*)

Yearning aloud can be a very beneficial experience for any
survivor, but because of the presence of other people, or the survivor's own reserve, it may be very difficult to do, if not impossible. If you wish to yearn, but are not able to do so overtly, you
can yearn intensely and unabashedly in writing. No one will
listen, watch, criticize, or analyze. In fact, your expression on
paper may border on the unintelligible, but that doesn't matter.
It's only important for you to express what you're feeling — that
you sorely miss, need, and cry out for your loved one.

Many survivors talk aloud to the pictures of their loved ones
for several months after the death. This kind of talking can be
done on paper as well. Such an exercise will allow you to let out
feelings that might otherwise be cut off by a belief that if you
pine for your loved one "too much" you will be in danger of
completely losing control or going crazy. By yearning in this way,
you can prove to yourself that those fears are unfounded. At the
same time, you can accept your loved one's death and reach a
full recognition of the *permanence* of the loss. Such recognition is
absolutely necessary for the successful resolution of the death.

And this is what life is to be forever? As it has been
for a year now — dominated by an absence, by days
full of chance reminders: the sight of some other child,
some inconsequential event that triggers a rush of
memories almost before I have had time to register it?
Facing every day dozens — hundreds? — of times, the
knowledge that they are gone and can never be
brought back; the knowledge that my need for them,
my yearning to have them with me, to hear and touch
them, are impulses that can never find fulfillment....

(John Tittensor, *Year One*)

To Explore

Death creates a void in your life which needs to be filled with something that can serve as a touchstone for your future. Depending upon your particular character and personality, death may change your image of yourself, your perception of the world, your religious convictions, your belief in other people, your understanding of what your purpose is in life, your feelings of belonging, your self-confidence, or your understanding of how you "fit" in the universe. Your loved one's death produced disorientation which is now likely to be compounded by emotional chaos in your life. If you wish, you can use writing to explore the variety of unfamiliar states and conditions which cause you any confusion. When you explore these turbulent emotional and intellectual territories, you can begin to focus your thoughts, to "place" yourself in the world, to get relief, and to produce in yourself some productive change. Some of the most common underlying questions which beg for answers are: *Who am I now? Where do I go from here? What is going on in this world? What's the "big picture" of my life? What role does God have now? Is there a God?*

After a death, you may change the way you perceive God or begin to question your other spiritual beliefs. A survivor may find renewed faith and solace in the reaffirmation of his belief in God; or a survivor may find himself ignoring or "boycotting" God, or doing some bargaining to make his life more livable in the future. Disillusionment about any number of things can motivate you to explore your feelings in writing. Any belief or value that has been taken away from you, warped, or changed, can create in you the necessity to put something in its place, to fill the gap, to make sense of its disappearance or destruction, and to be able to feel less distanced from your familiar belief system.

> I rehabilitated myself. My inner voice. My writing, my spiritual strivings were what rehabilitated me.
> *(40-year-old Vietnam vet)*

Because spirituality is the single dimension of life that goes beyond the physical, psychological, and social realms, it is the one which seems to be the most puzzling and which invites exploration — both before a loved one's death (as in the case of a terminal illness) and after the death. This dimension is closely linked to the void many survivors face after a loved one's death. Often, a survivor hopes to clarify his own identity by exploring the unknown. If so, he tries to grasp the "scheme" of things in this way. He tries to reach new insights that will give him some basis for understanding that which transcends all other aspects of his daily existence.

To Keep a Thorough Account of Your Grief

As you work through your loss, you can gain emotional comfort from keeping a private journal in which you record an in-depth, detailed account of your feelings, actions, observations, and fantasies. In other words, the daily journal can become a confidential repository for anything you think, do, and say during the day. By writing daily entries, you can consistently expiate and explore your various reactions. Such entries serve as a record to show you *what you have been through*. At any time, you can look back at where you were and how you felt, and then you can reflect upon any changes which are taking place. Even though your life may seem to consist of small segments of unfamiliar experience which have no predictable pattern, the journal can provide a safe territory in which you can examine your life as a whole.

Your journal does not criticize you, or demand anything from you. It does not care if you cry. It's there whenever you are moved to pick it up, to record any moment of your day that is particularly touching, disturbing, or conflicted.

Some survivors find that frequent letters to a loved one or friend can serve the same purpose as a daily journal.

> High clouds, a fine cool day, and this evening the rain
> has returned, with the comforting, steady drip from
> my leaky gutter which is clogged by fir needles. I only
> had one bad moment today: in the kitchen, a pretty
> ceramic mobile, of doves in flight, hangs by the
> window; Robin [a guest] touched it, and it rang gently,
> as the doves circled; the lump rose in my throat, as the

picture of Barbara hanging it, and often touching it, came back to me. I had washed the sheets and pillow cases, and re-made the bed, with just a faint smile of regret earlier, but the unexpected sight and sound of the flight of the doves slayed me.

(From the letters of a 64-year-old widower)

Survivors often gain courage and strength by reading the journals, letters, or poems written by others who have experienced losses similar to their own. In time of great emotional distress, another survivor's written word can serve as a kind of bond. It pulls the reader inside the net of shared sorrow and affirms, "Yes, I am in here too, and this is how it feels." Through honest, open writing, a survivor can share the complications and heartbreak of his loss with other survivors.

To "Keep" Your Loved One

Frequently, one of a survivor's strongest anxieties comes from his *fear of losing the memory of his loved one* — forgetting his voice, the way she looked, his gestures, her laugh — or *forgetting an emotional scene or an event* which occurred between himself and his loved one.

If you find yourself wishing you could hold onto everything you can possibly recall about your loved one and fearing that it won't be possible, you may like to try doing this: Write a full description of the person including every detail you can recall. Such a description will include all aspects of your loved one's personality, character, abilities, manner of speaking, gestures, habits, preferences, appearance, intelligence, humor, and so forth. For example, if you are grieving the loss of your wife, you may motivate your writing by answering questions similar to these: *What did I first notice about her? What impressed me most? What touched me most? What was it that made her unique, lovable, enjoyable to be with, interesting, challenging? What did we have between the two of us that no one else shared? Why? What made that possible?*

There may have been a particular emotional exchange between you and your loved one that you want to remember in vivid detail. Such a scene or an event may affirm the love you shared with the person who died; it may bring comfort to you, or it may assure you that you did nothing wrong in a certain situation. You may feel rather desperate about remembering a certain scene exactly, or you may even be obsessive about reviewing it: *Will I always remember that last conversation we had? Months from now, will I be able to remember our last trip together? Will I remember what happened before he left the night of the accident? Will I remember the talks my son and I had the last few days of his life? Will I remember the last time I made love to my wife? Or remember the special day my dad and I spent together before I knew he was sick?*

Such writing may also tell the story of a loved one's decline before his death, as was done in the following journal entry about the survivor's brother:

Todd came out of the doctor's office and told me, "Don't worry about you and Meg finding children to adopt. I think you're going to have our children to raise." Right after that he began to get real weak. He tried to keep working but it got harder and harder. He withdrew from people and didn't want to talk, would just sit and listen or watch TV. When people came to visit he tried to be nice to them, but I knew he wanted them to leave. He didn't want to be seen that way. It went on from June to September. It seemed like forever, all summer. He lost more and more weight. The last few weeks before he died, he was so small he wore David's [their youngest brother's] clothes. Even though he was twenty eight, he looked like an old man. Whenever I came out of his house I drove my truck down by the canal and cried before I could drive home. He was my big brother. He had looked out for me and believed in me. Now he was small and weak. Every night when I went to bed I wished for him to die....

(Brother of a cancer victim)

In the following poem the poet chronicles the decline and death of his cousin:

Diary of the Heart Attack

In December
the doctor swiveled his chrome chair forward
and from behind polished reserve he loosened years
from your grasp, froze your whole life
from the first haircut to receding hairline.
When you asked for evidence, he showed you
an exact picture of the clot aimed
like a bullet at your heart.

Driving from the doctor's office, you
studied a flashing dot on an aircraft tower,
wondered how far its light would travel
before invisibility swallowed it.
Then you accelerated, gained a small surge
of power over bad news and distance home.

In early June, you rose from half a bowl
of Wheaties and an empty orange juice glass;
with swelled hands and short breaths, you
trudged to the garage for tools
to weed the vegetable garden. Later,
you varnished a birch door recently hung
at the back of the house and cement-patched
cracks in the front porch steps.

With hot stickiness transforming your shirt
to a translucent skin, you worked steadily
throughout the day. Squatting to knees,
you clipped grass, manicured a line
along the driveway. About four-thirty,
the lawn, stippled with dandelion shadows, blurred
to yellow. Lips parted for a small gasp, lungs
tugging for oxygen, you leaned
into a curious bow, sliced into silence
glossy with sunlight, your empty hand
a foot from the clippers, your breath,
like a hummingbird, stopped in mid-air.

R. Nikolas Macioci

Some survivors agonize over fears of forgetting the death
scene, especially when its crucial to them to remember it because

some special sentiment or message was conveyed by their loved one, or some especially touching gesture was made, either silently or aloud. The person who died may have had a certain peacefulness or radiance or an intense, urgent quality or "seemed to be resigned." In such cases, the survivor may worry about the possibility of the memory slipping away as time goes on.

If you wish to preserve a scene or event, you may begin by asking: *Where were we at the time? Was I sitting, standing, walking, driving the car, lying down? What time of the day or night was it? What season? What were we wearing? Exactly what did he or she say? What did he or she do? How did I reply or respond? Exactly what did I do? How did I feel at the time? Was anyone else there? What did they do and say? How did I feel about it afterward?*

Once a scene or event is the subject of intense recollection, it will usually come into focus. As you write, words may tend to pour out, to gather momentum and incorporate many details. You may even feel as if the recollection is writing itself.

To Memorialize or Create

Closely related to writing which "keeps" the loved one is writing which honors the loved one and serves as a memorial. Such writing may take any form — journal entry, song, short story, or poem.

This type of writing is usually intended to be read and appreciated by others. It serves as a tribute or, as one writer put it, "a finely-polished remembrance of the person who died." Such a piece begins with the wish (or creative drive) to honor the loved one. At first, the writer may jot down a phrase or two, the first line of a song or poem, or the first paragraph of a story. As the piece grows, it is edited and shaped by the writer until he's pleased that his creation appropriately represents or pays tribute to his loved one. One writer explained that he began working on a story about his father when he couldn't sleep: "I sat alone at night in the kitchen pouring my father onto that paper. I tried to tell his story not in my voice but in his own voice. It was a way of keeping close to him and trying to make something with him in it, something tangible that would live after his death."

Other writers have done the same with stories, songs or poems. Below is an excerpt from a ten-part poem which was written after the death of the poet's friend.

He died in the Hospice
swaddled in wonderful white linen.
He died on a day when the sky
was a taut, electric blue dancing.
Molecules buzzing. All atoms everywhere
dancing, save in my friend.
For me, a stillness came over everything.
The wind stopped, birds sat blinking,
a vacuum touched everywhere.
Miles away men stopped their doings
and wondered why the silence.

He simply stopped breathing
In a coma for some time,
in shallow Cheyne-Stoke breathing,
He just forgot and stopped
and stared at eternity....

(Don Marsh, *An Ice Cream
Communion*)

This poet described the role the writing played in his life as
he grieved his friend's death.

The writing of the poem was an amazing experience...
a spiritual experience...It was very important that I
get it done. It was almost like an urgency that if I
don't get this done and I die, then it'll be wrong. I
have to do this. It was like the writing of that replaced
the other ritual of getting up to go to his house.
Instead of Vince in mind, it was getting up with the
poem in mind. And I would wake up and say, "Today,
I'm going to write the rage section," and I would do
it. It wrote itself in a relatively short period of time. I
did say to someone shortly after I wrote it... that it
really was almost as if I were taking dictation. It just
seemed to come out of me, and I had to get it done.
Somehow, the poem made another completion. It was
like saying, "See, Vince. This is my love on paper.
Formal, declared love that will live by itself." It's
my statement, a letter that says, "This is how much
I love this man."

Men who write to memorialize a loved one often describe being driven to the process. Some say it's the only way they knew to deal with what they were feeling. A survivor of parental and sibling death said, "I'll get the first verse of a poem, or the first few lines, or get the general feeling. Because once there's a feeling there, an emotion there, once the poem takes form, the emotion becomes very specific."

All grief-related writing does not necessarily come during the immediate period following the death. A survivor may write about his loss the next day and continue writing about it for a very long time, or he may not write anything at all for years and then suddenly find that writing is an appropriate and helpful outlet.

A man surviving the loss of his father wrote the following poem two years after the death.

In a Van Gogh December

The long broken limbs
of the greasewood
hang limp from the stove
My eyes burn and water
in the creosote smoke
that fills the small cabin
hot against winter chill

In the soil two years now
my father would have loved
today's cold clean blue
the wind howling wild
in the white writhe of poplar
the leaves letting go
into the wide wail of skyline
the yellow blood wheeling
out in great bursts
bereaving a worn wound.

Stephen Meadows

There is a compelled quality to such writing. It may range from explosive to quietly desperate, as reflected in the last lines of this poem which was written by another poet after the death of his father.

Dead Weight

My father lifted all his life —
limbs, stumps, loads of dirt
and gravel, rocks struck by the mower
and dug out with a full day's shoveling —
as if the balance of the planet
depended on his back.

He died lifting, pulling the weary beans
and tomatoes out of November by their roots
and pitching them armful by armful
into the woods at the end of the yard,
falling there heavily, too heavily,
clutching his chest as the sky tilted
and the trees leaned forward, darkening.

I finished the job he started,
uprooted the rest of the plants
and dropped them on his pile
at the edge of the brown tree line;
but that was not enough.
His dead weight became granite,
grew immense as quarries,
and the great globe wobbled,
its axis screaming for balance.
Desperate, I brought what I could carry:
these words piled here.

Neal Bowers

To "Build" Something

Up to this point, the various types of writing that have been discussed are ones which *directly* help a survivor through the grieving process. But there is still another type of writing that some survivors find both appropriate and possible after they have processed their grief. This kind of writing has a specific aim that involves others. It provokes, inspires, informs, motivates, requests, or calls to action. Generally, the survivor who is most likely to use the written word in this way is the one whose loved one was killed in an accident, murdered, or died of AIDS.

Somebody dies and you are shaken by his death. The death inspires you to write. Why? What is the meaning of your writing then? It is not simply that you are overburdened with grief — it is a protest. Instead of giving in to the grief, you take the grief and you say, "I shall build something with it." And then it becomes a protest against death.

(Elie Wiesel, *Against Silence*)

In such writing, a survivor may protest an injustice, plea for an investigation, propose a change in the law, urge others to begin a campaign, lobby for the banning of a harmful product, or solicit contributions for an individual, institution, or organization which has some relationship to the causes or circumstances of his loved one's death.

All of the types of writing presented here cover the basic avenues of grief. They are ways in which you can be withdrawn or silent and can still process your grief at the same time. While grieving that is done on paper is highly effective, it is important to note that utilizing *both* oral and written channels of release can be even more beneficial, especially in the immediate period following your loss.

11

Grieving and Male Companionship

*I don't apologize for crying. But I am glad there
are men around to help me fill the role I play in
my family life. That is something we do for one
another. The silent hand. The extended ladder. The
shrug that says, "I understand." The chance to be
"weak" and not be counted as weak at all. Brothers
recognizing that if we can't feel, then we are not
going to be good to anybody. And it's necesssary to
have brother and fathers in those times when it is
just not supposed to show.*

(ROGER WITHERSPOON, "SAY
BROTHER," *ESSENCE*)

One of the most valuable sources of support a man can have
following his loved one's death is the genuine friendship and
companionship of another man or other men. A survivor may
have the support and comfort of women, but within that nurturing relationship, regardless of how generous and intense it is, one
special and important component is missing: the acceptance of
the male survivor's grief-related behavior by another man.

Unfortunately, many men do not form any solid, close male
friendships. In Daniel J. Levinson's *The Seasons of a Man's Life*, he
underscored this fact when he noted the limited relationships of
his male interviewees.

In our interviews, friendship was largely noticeable by its absence. As a tentative generalization we would say that close friendship with a man or woman is rarely experienced by American men....A man may have a wide social network in which he has amicable, "friendly" relationships with many men and perhaps a few women. In general, however, most men do not have an intimate male friend of the kind that they recall fondly from boyhood or youth....We need to understand why friendship is so rare, and what consequences this deprivation has for adult life.

The Origin and Nature of Men's Relationships

It is reasonable to pursue the question, "Why is friendship rare?" Looking at the origins of men's isolation helps to identify ways in which it can change.

Boys' Relationships

Researchers have noted that young boys play in larger groups, groups of three or four; girls, on the other hand, more often have one playmate, which allows them to engage in one-to-one interaction. As a result, girls establish a closeness with one another. It is interesting to note, also, that boys' play is more frequently focused on an object or an activity, while girls' play is focused on an interaction between people. There's a dispute among scientists as to whether this behavior is genetic or a product of cultural conditioning. Is it, some ask, that we expect and encourage girls to be more person-oriented and more nurturing?

The important point as it relates to the absence of strong friendships between men is that the lack of such a one-to-one relationship does not manifest itself only in the adult years. In fact, the lack is observable among very young children. Studies of children at play revealed that boys exhibit a propensity for creating high structures like forts which shut out, structures with walls and facades, with protrusions and "cannons." Boys' play reflects a tendency to protect the self, to keep separate from other people. Automobiles, animals and objects are placed on the *outside* of the constructions. In contrast, girls' scenes are *interior*, with simple enclosures, low walls, and a doorway here and there. Such scenes are relatively peaceful and may be considered inclusive. The girls' tendency is to have a more open environment which does not seem to need to shut out, or protect against invasion.

As males and females mature, it's evident that girls form strong bonds in pairs, and that boys interact in groups or gangs. These male relationships tend to discourage exchanges, bonding, or intimacy.

The Nature of Men's Relationships

> Society teaches us to separate from our emotional, physical, and social nature and to behave according to the rules of a profession. Under such regulations, one performs increasingly limited rational operations, whether it is a matter of cutting up a body or a poem, a market profile or a mass of computations. Successful people in this system are able to perform reliably over a long period of time. Very successful people also manage somehow, to preserve the outer show of charisma, charm, magnetism, or whatever other qualities are conducive to being trusted and assigned leadership roles. In every case, however, the result is the same: one identifies with a socially cultivated mask the essential character of which is its lack of human depth and, most especially, its lack of depth of feeling. Can people under such discipline be true friends?
>
> (Stuart Miller, *Men and Friendship*)

In a study conducted with unmarried college students, investigators surveyed men and women to find out to what degree they told others of their disappointments and feelings of failure, and to what degree other people confided personal feelings to them. The study determined that women confided more, and were confided in more often.

Men tend not to be intimate. They don't really know
what's going on...in the workings of the mind and
heart of their friend. They don't really know that.
When asked, they draw a blank. They might know
how the person plays cards, or what football team they
like...things like that, but they don't really know the
inner workings of the person. They don't know how
that person might want to die, for example.

(37-year-old men's group facilitator)

Traditionally, men's relationships have been built on activities (making something, selling something, transporting
something, fixing something, refining a product, preparing a campaign, organizing a team, and so forth) or they have been built
around functions (employers and employees, teachers and students, officers and enlisted men, ministers and parishioners, and
so on); or men have banded together against a competitor — the
other fraternity, the other team, the other business, the other
country.

One-to-one relationships are culturally approved among
men if they're done while in the process of *doing something else* —
hunting, fishing, or drinking, for example. We all know how
prominent a part liquor plays in much of men's companionship.
If we should forget for a moment, all we need to do is turn on
the television and the beer commercials will quickly remind us.
Goldberg says, in *The New Male*, "Perhaps because of their great
anxiety about intimacy or closeness with other males, or the fear
of transparency, men seem to require liquor in order to relax
when socializing with associates. They meet at bars or in a
restaurant over a drink and then proceed to drink continuously
while they are together."

The rules say that it's okay to go hiking with Ted, or have
a beer with Frank, but it's less acceptable to just go see Ted in
order to sit down and share meaningful personal concerns or feelings, or to ask Frank to come over for the purpose of talking.

When closeness does occur, it's more likely to happen during
a very safe time. It is also more probable that it will occur in a
neutral environment, instead of on anyone's home turf. Getting
away for a shared activity can signal a release, as if to say, "We're
away from what we *must* be most of the time. On this common

ground, for which neither of us is responsible, we can now open up and share."

> I should say right here that Larry and I have been fishing together for most of our adult lives which means we have sorted out the significance of our respective triumphs and failures, have seen each other through career crises, divorces, what have you. We have learned to read each other. So we know when enough distance has passed under the wheels, when the time is right, when it is safe to turn the radio down and do what we cannot do until we're going fishing. We talk.
>
> We ask indirectly, and in so many words: Why did our parents withhold praise from us while passing along favors to our siblings? Why do our wives and children forget we have feelings? Why is it always up to us to be calm and wise? Why does everyone make us feel so guilty? Why is it that we are misunderstood by the people we love? Why can't we escape our mothers? Why do sentimentaliy and melancholy and loneliness prevail over our natural inclination to be playful? Why, in the end, does it take us so long to learn that things are the way they are and always will be? When will we be able to quit asking these questions that we have asked each other a hundred times before during dozens of fishing trips?
>
> Still, we listen deferentially and provide quiet, abstract answers that don't appear much like answers at all, only comforting sounds of male bonding....
>
> ...Larry and I have bonded with each other, in fishing, in clowning around, in catastrophes and, occasionally, even in tears. We are bonded because we offer something to each other that most of the rest of our world does not, and that is safety.
>
> (Patrick Dillon, "The Healing Place," WEST, San Jose Mercury News)

When men survivors were asked what they want most from a friendship with another man, the qualities they most frequently named were acceptance, honesty, and understanding. The "second string" of desirable requirements were compassion, sensitivity, and dependability.

An interview with Stan, a vet's counselor, points up, typically, men's desire for total acceptance.

Interviewer: Who is your closest male friend?

Stan: An Army buddy.

Interviewer: What qualities make him a candidate for your close friendship — more than someone else you're close to?

Stan: He's my friend, no matter what I do.

Interviewer: Acceptance, then?

Stan: Yes, acceptance. No judgment, no matter what I do. And if I was in trouble and needed to depend on someone, I could depend on him. And also, he could depend on me. Even if it means to really put our *whole trip* on the line.

All of the qualities identified as being most needed and desirable in a close man friend are the ones most appreciated by a grieving man, and foremost among them are acceptance, understanding, and compassion.

> ...in friendship we are curiously drawn by the other man's inner beauty past the reflexive aversion to his outer appearance. We are drawn by his wit, the set of his eyes that makes us think we are seen. We are drawn by his apparent gentleness, his directness, his valor. We are drawn by his energy, a male force we share and that reinforces ours just when the world and time seem to have flattened us out altogether. Past the shaggy-beast exterior, the threatening otherness that is also our own physical self, we find a heart that beats with ours, a brain that chimes with ours, an understanding that includes the same masculinity that is, too often, a burden in this life.
>
> (Stuart Miller, *Men and Friendship*)

Providing Emotional Support

When a man suffers the loss of a loved one, he can benefit greatly from having a close male friend who is able to do any one, or more, of the following:

- Acknowledge the death.
- Express genuine interest in the survivors *real* feelings, concerns, and conditions.
- Be completely trustworthy in regard to confidences.
- Accept, even encourage, tears.
- Share a silence in which the survivor and friend communicate nonverbally.
- Perform incidental acts of compassion.

Acknowledging the Death

Many men complain about being avoided or ignored by friends after the death. They are treated, as one survivor put it, "as if I had some terrible communicable disease." Then he added, "I guess I did. The disease called death." When other people turn away, the loneliness of the survivor intensifies.

> I was alone that weekend. Female friends came to visit Mary in the hospital. They hugged her, talked to her, allowed her to cry. Men didn't come to see me, to let me cry and tell them how I felt. How was I to grieve over this loss? Men don't comfort each other during these painful times, but I am sure most men must have feelings similar to those I felt. Later, men told me they had seen me and turned away because they didn't know how to react or what to say.
> (Steve Laroe, "My Infant's Death: A Father's Story," *Glamour*)

A father who lost his teenaged son in an auto accident told of his fury when old friends who saw him in public turned and went the other way. He recalled how appreciative he was when an acquaintance came up to him in a service station, gripped his hand, and simply said, "Damn, it's the shits, isn't it?" The point here is, of course, that expressions of sympathy don't have to be eloquent, but they must be heartfelt. The expression must acknowledge the other person's pain and convey honesty. It is certainly hurtful and dishonest for a friend or acquaintance to pretend he isn't conscious of the death the survivor has just gone through. Ignoring the death ignores the person. It invalidates him. It gives him the disquieting message, "You'll be what you *have* to be, but you won't be *you*."

Expressing an Interest in Feelings, Concerns, and Conditions

In addition to acknowledging the death, a friend or companion should express an interest in what is going on emotionally and mentally with the survivor. During a phone call or a visit over coffee, or while spending some other time alone, the survivor can be gently and respectfully invited to express what's on his mind and in his heart.

> A neighbor, Don, came to the house while I was on the phone. He waited in the backyard. We sat on a pile of wood as he asked how I was doing. Did I want to talk about what happened? I started to talk, my eyes filling with tears. But I still felt afraid to cry in front of him.
> (Steve Laroe, "My Infant's
> Death: A Father's Story,"
> *Glamour*)

A thirty-seven-year-old painter gave one reason for appreciating the friend who supported him after the death of his father. "He *listens*. He really hears what's being said, and we have a long history together. I told him, told him all I had to say the best I could. And he *listened*."

It is extremely important for the listener to accept the survivor's expressions which reflect conflict, as well as more focused, and less complex feelings. A survivor's reactions are often mixed, even seemingly contradictory. A good listener hears it all and accepts the "socially unacceptable" remarks on equal terms with the socially acceptable. Such a friend provides simple, unelaborate verbal support. An ordinary comment such as "It's hard to have both of those feelings battling with one another," or "It's not easy to put a label on something as painful as grief or to figure it all out" can be of tremendous value to the receptive griever.

Being Trustworthy in Regard to Confidences

Of course, an untrustworthy listener is worse than no listener at all. A man's grief involves his deepest, most private feelings. Sometimes these feelings may come in the form of revelations which would not be released under any other circumstances: "My wife wasn't faithful to me," or "I always felt my wife loved our child more than me," or "I hated my father all his life for the way he treated my sister and me. I used to wish he'd die." When a survivor's dialogue takes the turn toward self-disclosure, a companion can provide assurance and support by saying something that lets the survivor know his confidences will not be betrayed. For example, he may say "I appreciate that you trust me to listen and to care," or "Some of our feelings are so private, we don't realize that *we don't have to hold them in.*" If the companion has a similar experience, he might briefly refer to it or share it when it's clear the survivor has finished his own story.

Accepting Tears

A man who survived the suicide of his teenaged daughter was asked what qualities he valued most in a male friend. He answered, "One who can express, and essentially receive, the same kinds of feelings that I have. Almost all of my male friends are that way. None of them would be ashamed if I were to cry in front of them, nor would I be ashamed to watch them experience their grief in front of me. And yet all of them have qualities that are very male. With the men I know and value, there is a very outward expression of emotion."

I think people who develop a real friendship are men
who have been very badly hurt and unconsciously go
to that most exact of all human places to heal
themselves. In some complicated way, friendship at its
most perfect is related to deep suffering and deep
illness; the acute horror of being forced into desolation
by a society that clearly has little real interest in
human values. So when people go toward each other
and love one another, there's a kind of deep, deep
medication. Real friendship, then, is a kind of divine
act that enables two people to share feelings, to have
feelings that life denies continually.

(Stuart Miller, *Men and Friendship*)

The Vietnam vet (in chapter 9) who described his experience
of crying for the first time in the vets' support group emphasized
how men encouraged one another to cry if they felt like it: "Hey,
I hear you man. It's like your throat is closing up and you feel
like you're going to cry." Such support can be shown in the same
way in a one-to-one relationship. The survivor will benefit by
hearing that crying is okay; it goes along with what is happening
emotionally or verbally, and it isn't going to make anybody uncomfortable. When a man is struggling to hold back tears, he'll
be relieved to hear a quiet "You don't have to keep it in, you
know."

Sharing a Silence

A lot has been said, thus far, about the real need to break
through silence, to talk about grief, and to express feelings. Of
course, this is crucially important. But it would be restrictive and
incorrect to ignore the ways that sorrow, despair, vulnerability
and other grief-related feelings can be communicated without em-
ploying words.

I told him I wanted to be alone. But it wasn't true. I
just didn't want to talk. I did want men around, even
if I didn't cry in front of them. Even if I didn't say a
damn thing. Just be there. Share the sorrow with me
and help me be as 'strong' as I think I ought to be for

my wife, when in reality I would very much like to
fold.

(Roger Witherspoon, "Say,
Brother," *Essence*)

There are times — rare, poignant times, usually — when a
very simple gesture, a certain look, a nod, touch, or pat, conveys
everything the other person needs to know.

We've all had the experience of someone repeating a conversation and then adding, "It wasn't what he said, it was how he
said it." "How he said it," usually refers to body language as well
as tone of voice. How we look, breathe and move — whether we
slouch, lean forward, gaze off into space, or shift our feet — all
tend to convey our emotions. The grieving person picks up similar cues from other people, cues that say, "It's okay to be down-
cast," or "Your lack of concentration is understandable," or "I
don't expect you to respond," or, "Here, let me do that for you,"
or "I know. This is pure hell," or any number of other messages.

James J. Lynch, in *The Broken Heart: The Medical Consequences
of Loneliness*, tells of observations he made in a coronary care unit.

One of [the elementary facts about life] is our basic
need to communicate. When someone's life is in mortal
peril, this need is stripped of all its usual complexity
and is expressed most directly through simple acts like
holding hands. Having watched many people visit
their loved ones in coronary care units, I have been
struck by the way that most people finally say
good-bye...it is almost as if some deep, primitive,
instinctive ritual takes over. Surprisingly, many wives
do not kiss their husbands good-bye, as if they were
afraid that such contact might hurt their ill mate. But
just before leaving, they will stop speaking and silently
hold the patient's hand or touch his body or even
stand at the foot of the bed and hold the patient's foot.
The contact is brief, yet deeply poignant. More often
than not, the final good-bye does not involve words,
almost as if words alone were insufficient to
communicate their true feelings. The most simple and
direct type of human communicaton does not need
words.

Performing Small Acts of Compassion

At work, the survivor can be helped by co-workers doing something to ease his daily load. During grief, the majority of survivors will feel overwhelmed. Any help that can be provided which will save the survivor's energy and effort should be considered. Taking over a task quietly, efficiently, and without any fanfare, is one of the most effective ways to help. Making a public announcement of good intentions removes the sincerity and validity of the gesture.

Providing Practical Assistance

While a male friend can provide crucial emotional support to a survivor, practical assistance may also be very badly needed. But this need may be overlooked by those who are focusing on the general circumstances into which a friend or relative has been catapulted following his loved one's death. For the survivor truly *is* catapulted into a morass of responsibilities, requests for decisions, paperwork, and a stream of tedious, time-consuming, and often confusing details. Most of the tasks following the death of a loved one were, until recently, expected to be carried out by the man in the family, or by some other male. Now, however, in a growing number of families there is a fairly equal sharing among the adults of all the postdeath duties.

It cannot be emphasized too often that a man who has recently suffered a loss feels immense appreciation when other men pitch in to help. Men who have experienced such help from friends remark on how deeply touched they were by the solid bond of brotherhood that seemed to instantly appear just when they needed it most. A father who survived the suicide of his teenager was moved to tears as he recalled the genuine assistance he received from his friends the morning after the tragedy.

> The next morning three of my colleagues came over to the house, and they all offered their services. You name it, we'll do it...and they did. One of them took care of finding a gravesite...and this...this is marvelous to have friends like that.

There are inumerable things another man (or woman) can do to ease the burden of the survivor and his family.

- Make a preliminary call to a priest, minister, or rabbi for purposes of arranging a service.

- Call a funeral director.

- Call relatives and friends of the survivor who need to be notified.

- Call the survivor's place of employment and give instructions about what information should be disseminated to other employees.

- Find a gravesite or get information about cremation.

- Help compile information for the funeral notice in the paper or find out in what form it is needed and when it is to be received by the paper.

- Help arrange for the memorial donations. Find out the address of the recipient organization chosen by the survivor and see that it gets listed in the funeral notice.

- Accompany the survivor as he takes the deceased's clothing to the funeral director or as he tackles other emotionally demanding tasks.

- Provide transportation or housing for relatives and friends attending the services from out of town.

- If there is to be a gathering at home after the service, see about getting special items that may be required, such as additional chairs or a large coffee maker, and so on.

In addition to the tasks which relate directly to the funeral service, there are numerous ways to relieve the many pressures caused by the urgency of the situation and to provide the type of help that substitutes order for disorder.

- Field incoming telephone calls.

- Watch the house if the family will be going to another town for the services.

- Mow the lawn before visitors arrive, or arrange to have it cared for.

- Do grocery shopping.

- Take the car and get it washed and waxed.

- Take clothes to the cleaners.

Any man who genuinely wants to help another has only to look and listen, so he can *see* and *hear* what needs to be done. Then he arranges to do it. When a man says to a survivor, "Call me if you need me," before he hangs up the telephone or walks away, it's the same as saying, "See what a nice guy I am? Goodbye." A man who is grieving needs more than offered support, he needs proof that support exists.

As one man accompanies another through the first task-filled days of his loss, and on through his grief—for weeks and then months—it is important for the survivor's companion to maintain trust in the grieving process. It may occasionally be necessary for the friend to understand the survivor's silence as well as his need to talk, his withdrawal as well as his ready acceptance of fellowship, his occasional unexplainable behavior or his apparent disinterest in things about which he was once enthusiastic.

When the survivor grows weary or disillusioned with his own efforts to work through his loss, it's important for him to be reminded that no man's grieving can be condensed or resolved easily or quickly. During particularly trying times, a survivor's friend may need to encourage him to have faith and belief in his own process, even though he may not see or feel noticeable gains, and to be assured that grief which is worked through will eventually be resolved.

When the loss *is* being resolved, there will be some evidence of it. The survivor will be able to speak of his loved one without experiencing great overwhelming sadness or desperation. He will use the past tense when talking about the person and will not struggle to maintain control over what he is saying or how he is saying it. He will express a genuine interest in activities and people and will be able to participate at work and in social situations with relative ease. He will even be able to smile and laugh.

Each *day* of working through his grief is a *step toward* the survivor's emergence from his forest of unhappiness and despair.

He will reenter the world a changed man who leaves behind the severest emotional pains of his loss. While there will still be the challenge of going forward without a loved one, that challenge will be met within a meaningful life—one that holds the promise of participation, pleasure, reward and continuing love.

"Men's Initiation Rites" by Robert Bly. Published in *Utne Reader*, April/May 1986. Reprinted with permission of Robert Bly.

"Diary of a Heart Attack" by R. Nikolas Macioci. Published by The New Press, Spring 1991. Reprinted with permission of Nik Macioci.

"Say, Brother," by Roger Witherspoon. Copyright 1983 by *Essence* magazine. Reprinted with permission of Roger Witherspoon.

Year One by John Tittensor. Copyright 1984 by Mc Phee Gribble Publishers. Reprinted with permission of Mc Phee Gribble Publishers and John Tittensor.

The Bereaved Parent, by Harriet Schiff. Copyright 1977 by Harriet Sarnoff Schiff. Reprinted by permission of Crown Publishers.

Manhood by Stephen A. Shapiro. Copyright 1985 by Stephen A. Shapiro. Reprinted with permission of the Putnam Publishing Group.

"Similiarities and differences in mothers' and fathers' grief following the death of an infant," by A. Dyregrov and Stig Berge Mattheissen, published in *Scandanavian Journal of Psychology*. Copyright 1987 by Almqvist and Wiksell International and reprinted with their permission.

"Goodbye" by Fred Wistow, published in *Family Therapy Networker*. Copyright 1986 by Family Therapy Networker and reprinted with their permission.

"Loss Reactions of College Students: A descriptive analysis," published in *Death Education*, Vol. 5., 1981. Copyright 1981 by Hemisphere Publishing Corporation. Reprinted with permission of Taylor and Francis, Hemisphere Publishing Corporation.

Recovering From the Loss of a Child by Katherine Fair Donnelly. Copyright 1982 by Katherine Fair Donnelly. Reprinted with permission of Macmillan Publishing Company.

On Children and Death by Elisabeth Kubler-Ross. Copyright 1983 by Elisabeth-Kubler Ross, M.D. Reprinted with permission of Macmillan Publishing Company.

"My Infant's Death: A Father's Story" by Steve Laroe, published in *Glamour* magazine. Copyright 1986 by Conde Nast Publications, Incorporated. Reprinted with permission of Steve Laroe.

Marriage and Divorce: A Social and Economic Study by Hugh Carter and Paul Glick. Published by Harvard University Press, copyright 1970.

"A Men's Group Story" by David Guy. Copyright 1989 by *The Independent*, Durham, North Carolina and reprinted with their permission.

A Savage God: A Study of Suicide by A. Alvarez, published by Random House. Copyright 1970, 1971 and 1972 by A. Alvarez. Reprinted with permission of George Weidenfeld and Nicolson Limited.

"Dead Weight" by Neal Bowers published in *Southern Poetry Review*. Copyright 1987 by *Southern Poetry Review* and reprinted with their permission.

Bibliography

Allen, Jon G. and Haccoun Markiewicz. "Sex differences in emotionality: A multi-dimensional approach," *Human Relations*, Vol. 29(8), 1976.

Alvarez, A. *The Savage God*. New York: Random House, 1970.

Axelrod, Julius, and Terry D. Reisne. "Stress hormones: Their interaction and regulation." *Science*, Vol 22(4), May 4, 1984.

Baechler, Jean. *Suicides*. New York: Basic Books. 1979.

Beck, Aaron T., M.D. *Depression: Clinical, Experimental and Theoretical Aspects*. New York: Harper and Row, 1967.

Beck, Aaron T., Robert A. Steer, Maria Kovacs, and Betsy Garrison. Hopelessness and eventual suicide: A 10 year prospective study of patients hospitalized with suicidal ideation." *American Journal of Psychiatry*, Vol 142, May 1985.

Bergstrom, Mark. "A father's grief for daughter turns to anger." *Santa Cruz Sentinel*, June 11, 1989.

Berlinsky, Ellen B., and Henry B. Biller. *Parental Death and Psychological Development*. Massachusetts: D.C. Heath and Company, 1982.

Blazer, D., D. Hughes and L.K. George. "Stressful life events and the onset of a generalized anxiety syndrome," *The American Journal of Psychiatry*, Vol. 144 (9), 1987.

Bly, Robert "Men's Initiation Rites," *Utne Reader*, April/May 1986.

Bolton, C. and D.J. Camp. "Funeral rituals and facilitation of grief work." *Omega*, Vol. 17(4). 1986-87.

Bowlby, John. *Attachment and Loss*, 2 vols. New York: Basic Books, 1969-1973.

_____ *Attachment and Loss*. Vol. III. London: Hogarth Press, 1980.

Burks, Valerie K., Dale A. Lund, Charles H. Gregg, and Harry P. Bluhm. "Bereavement and remarriage for older adults," *Death Studies*, Vol. 12(1), 1988.

Cain, Albert C. *Survivors of Suicide*. Illinois: Charles C. Thomas, 1972.

Calabrese, J.R., M.D; M.A. Kling, M.D.; and P.W. Gold, M.D. "Alterations in immunocompetence during stress, bereavement and depression: focus on neuroendocrine regulation." *American Journal of Psychiatry*, Vol. 144(9), 1987.

Calhoun, L.G., C.B. Abernathy, and J.W. Selby. "The rules of bereavement: Are suicidal deaths different?" *Journal of Community Psychology*, Vol.14(2), 1986.

Carter, Hugh and Paul C. Glick, *Marriage and Divorce: A Social and Economic Study*. Massachusetts: Harvard University Press, 1970.

Cole, Diane. "It might have been: Mourning the unborn." *Psychology Today*, July 1987.

Cornwell, Joanne B., Barry Nucombe M.D., and Leslie Stevens. "Family response to loss of a child by sudden infant death syndrome," *The Medical Journal of Australia*, April 30, 1977.

Dewey II, Denman. "When a congregation cares: Organizing ministry to the bereaved." *Death Studies*, Vol. 12, 1988.

Dillon, Patrick. "The Healing Place, *WEST, San Jose Mercury News.* January 26, 1985.

Doka, K.J. "Loss upon Loss: The impact of death after divorce," *Death Studies,* Vol. 10 (5), 1986.

_____ "Silent sorrow: grief and the loss of others." *Death Studies*, Vol. 11, 1987.

Donnelly, Katherine Fair. *Recovering From The Loss Of A Child.* New York: Macmillan, 1982.

Dosser, David A. Jr., Jack O. Balswick, and Charles F. Halverson Jr. "Situational context of emotional expressiveness." *Journal of Counseling Psychology.* Vol. 3(3), 1983.

Dullia, Georgia. "Widowers and their grieving." *New York Times*, September 12, 1983.

Durkheim, E. *Suicide: A Study in Sociology.* Trans. John A. Spaulding and George Simpson. Glencoe: The Free Press, 1951.

Dyregrov, A. and Stig Berge Mattheisen. "Similarities and differences in mothers' and fathers' grief following the death of an infant," *Scandanavian Journal of Psychology*, Vol.28(1), 1987.

Edelstein, Linda. *Maternal Bereavement.* New York: Praeger Publishers, 1984.

Ehrenreich, Barbara. *The Hearts of Men.* New York: Doubleday, 1983.

Emery, Gary. *A New Beginning.* New York: Simon and Schuster, 1981.

Fienson, M.C. "Aging widows and widowers: Are there mental health differences?" *International Journal of Aging and Human Development.* Vol. 23(4), 1986.

Fleming, Joan, and Sol Altschul. "Activation of mourning and growth by psychoanlaysis." *International Journal of Psychoanalysis*, Vol. 44, 1963.

Fletcher, J.C. and M.I. Evans. "Maternal bonding in early fetal ultrasound examinations." *New England Journal of Medicine*, Vol. 308, 1983.

Franklin, Clyde W. II. The Changing Definition of Masculinity, New York and London: Plenum Press, 1984.

Furman, Erna. *A Child's Parent Dies.* New Haven and London: Yale University, 1974.

Furman, R.A. "A child's capacity for mourning." *The Child in His Family: The Impact of Disease and Death.* ed. E.J. Anthony and C. Koupernick, New York: Wiley, 1973.

Gans, Adrienne "The war and peace of the Vietnam memorials," *American Imago*, Vol. 44 (4), 1987.

Geis, S.B., R.L. Fuller and J. Rush, "Lovers of AIDS victims: Psychosocial stresses and counseling needs." *Death Studies*. Vol. 10 (1), 1986.

Goldberg, Herb *The Hazards of Being Male*. New York: New American Library, 1976.

_____ *The New Male*. New York: New American Library, 1980.

Goodwin, J. "The etiology of combat-related post traumatic stress disorders." *Readjustment Problems Among Vietnam Veterans*, Disabled American Veterans (Pamphlet).

Gove, W.R. "The Relationship Between Sex Roles, Marital Status and Mental Illness." *Social Forces*, Vol. 51(1), 1972.

Greenberg, Samuel I. "Managing the potentially suicidal patient." *Physician and Patient*, Vol. 3., Feb. 1984.

Guy, David. "A men's group story." *The Independent*, Durham, North Carolina, 1989.

Honeycutt, James M., Charmaine Wilson and Christine Parker. "Effects of sex and degrees of happiness on perceived styles of communicating in and out of the marital relationship." *Journal of Marriage and the Family*, May 1982.

Howard, Stephen. M.D. "The Vietnam Warrior: His Experience and Implications for Psychotherapy." *American Journal of Psychotherapy*, Vol. 30(1), 1976.

Hendin, Herbert. *Suicide in America*. New York: W.W. Norton and Company, 1982.

Holliday, Laurel. *The Violent Sex*. California: Bluestocking Books, 1978.

Izard, Carroll E. *Patterns of Emotions*. New York: Academic Press, 1972.

Jacobs, Jerry. *Adolescent Suicide*. New York: John Wiley and Sons, 1971.

Jahr, Cliff. *A Voice for Today*. Parade Magazine, June 9, 1985.

Johnson, Robert J., Dale A. Lund, and Margaret F. Dimond. "Stress, self esteem and coping during bereavement among the elderly," *Social Psychology Quarterly*, Vol. 49(3), 1986.

Kennell, J. H. Slyter, and M. Klaus. "The mourning response of parents to the death of a newborn infant." *New England Journal of Medicine*, Vol. 283, 1970.

Kirkley-Best, E., and K. Kellner. "The forgotten grief: a review of the psychology of stillbirth." *American Journal of Orthopsychiatry*, Vol. 52, 1982.

Klass, D. "Marriage and divorce among bereaved parents in a self help group," *Omega*, Vol. 17 (3). 1986.

Klein, Sandra Jacoby, and William Fletcher. "Gay grief: An examination of its uniqueness brought to light by the AIDS crisis." *Journal of Psychosocial Oncology*, Vol. 4 (3), Fall 1986.

Knight, Albert F. "The Death of a Son." *New York Times Magazine*, June 22, 1986.

Knapp, Ronald J. "When A Child Dies," *Psychology Today*, July 1987.

Koestenbaum, Peter. *Managing Anxiety*. New Jersey: Prentice-Hall, Inc., 1974.

Krementz, Jill. *How It Feels When A Parent Dies*. New York: Alfred A. Knopf, 1981.

Kubler-Ross, Elisabeth. *On Death and Dying*. New York: Alfred A. Knopf, 1981.

_____*Questions and Answers on Death and Dying*. New York: Macmillan, 1974.

_____*On Children and Death*. New York: Macmillan, 1983.

La Grand, L.E. "Loss reactions of college students: A descriptive analysis." *Death Education*, Vol. 5., 1981.

Laroe, Steve. "My Infant's Death: A Father's Story." *Glamour*, April 1986.

Lee, John. *The Flying Boy*. Florida: Health Communications, Inc., 1987.

Legg, C., and I. Sherick. "The replacement child — a developmental tragedy: some preliminary comments." *Child Psychiatry and Human Development*, Vol. 7., 1976.

Levinson, Daniel J. *The Seasons Of A Man's Life*. New York: Alfred A. Knopf, 1978.

Leviton, D., "Thanatological theory and my dying father." *Omega*, Vol. 17 (2). 1986-87.

Lewis, C.S. *A Grief Observed*. New York: Bantam Seabury Press, 1963.

Lewis, Helen Block. *Psychic War In Men and Women*. New York: New York University Press, 1976.

Lieberman, E.J., M.D., "War and the family; the psychology of antigrief." *Modern Medicine*, April 19, 1971.

_____. "American Families and the Vietnam War." *Journal of Marriage and the Family*, November 1971.

Lindemann, E., "Symptamatology and management of acute grief." *American Jounal of Psychiatry*, Vol. 101, 1944.

Lochner, Charles W. and Stevenson, Robert G. "Music as a bridge To wholeness," *Death Studies*, Vol. 12, 1988.

Lofland, L.H. "The social shaping of emotion: The case of grief." *Symbolic Interaction*, Vol.8 (2), 1985.

Lonetto, Richard. *Children's Concepts of Death*. New York: Springer Publishing Company, 1980.

Lord, Janice Harris. "Survivor grief following a drunk driving crash," *Death Studies*. Vol. 11, 1987.

Lund, Dale A., *Older Bereaved Spouses: Research with Practical Applications*. New York: Hemisphere Publishing Corporation, 1989.

_____. Michael S. Caserta, and Margaret F. Dimond. "Effectiveness of self help groups for older bereaved spouses." Paper presented at the 42nd annual meeting of the Gerontological Society of American, Minneapolis, Minnesota, November 17-21, 1989.

_____. Michael S. Caserta, and Margaret Dimond, "Gender differences through two tears of bereavement among the elderly," *The Gerontologist*. 1986.

_____. Michael S. Caserta, Margaret Dimond, R.M. Gray. "Impact of bereavement on the self-conceptions of older surviving spouses." *Symbolic Interaction*, Vol. 9 (2), 1986.

_____. Michael S. Caserta, Jan Van Pelt, Kathleen A. Gass. "Stability of social support networks after later-life spousal bereavement." *Death Studies*, Vol.14, 1990.

Lynch, James J. M.D., *The Broken Heart: The Medical Consequences of Loneliness*. New York: Basic Books, 1976.

Lynn, David B. "Sex role and parental identification." *Child Development*, Vol. 33, 1962.

Maccoby, Eleanor Emmons, and Carol Nagy Jacklin. *The Psychology of Sex Differences*. Stanford: Stanford University Press, 1974.

Macon, L. "Help for bereaved parents." *Social Casework: The Journal of Contemporary Social Work*. November, 1979.

Maddison, D.C., and A. Viola. "The health of widows in the year following bereavement." *Journal of Psychosomatic Research*, Vol. 12, 1968.

Mauritzen, John. "Pastoral care for the dying and bereaved." *Death Studies*, Vol. 12, 1988.

May, Gerald G., M.D., *Addiction and Grace*, San Francisco: HarperCollins Publishers, 1988.

Mc Kay, Matthew, and Patrick Fanning. *Self-Esteem*. Oakland: New Harbinger Publications, 1986.

_____, Peter D. Rogers, and Judith McKay, *When Anger Hurts*. Oakland: New Harbinger Publications, 1989.

Menninger, Karl A. *Man Against Himself*. New York: Harcourt, Brace and Co. 1938.

Miller, Marv. *Suicide After Sixty*. New York: Springer Publishing Company, 1979.

Miller, Stuart. *Men and Friendship*, Boston: Houghton Mifflin Company, 1983.

Montague, Ashley. *Touching: The Human Significance of the Skin*. New York: Harper and Row, 1971.

Moore, Timothy E. and Reet Mae, "Who dies and who cries: Death and bereavement in children's literature," *Journal of Communications*, 37(4), Autumn. 1987

Morin, Stephen, F. and Walter F. Batchelor. "Responding to the psychological crisis of AIDS," *Public Health Reports*, Vol.99(1) 1984.

Murphy, Patricia Ann, "Parental death in childhood and loneliness in young adults," *Omega*, Vol. 17(3), 1986.

Notarius, Clifford I., and Jennifer S. Johnson. "Emotional expression in husbands and wives," *Journal of Marriage and the Family*, Vol. 44(2), May 1982.

Osterweis, Marian. "Bereavement and the elderly." *Aging*, U.S. Dept of Health and Human Services, 1985.

_____, Frederic Solomon, and Morris Green, eds. *Bereavement: Reaction, Consequences, and Care*. Washington, D.C.: National Academy Press, 1984.

Parks, Betty. "We waited seven years for a murder trial," *Survivors Newsletter*, Vol. IV(1), August, 1984.

Parkes, Colin Murray. *Bereavement*. London: Tavistock, 1972.

_____. Murray, B. Benjamin, and R.G. Fitzgerald. "Broken heart: a statistical study of increased mortality among widows and widowers." *British Medical Journal*, Vol. 1, 1969.

Parson, E.R. "Life after death: Vietnam veteran's struggle for meaning and recovery." *Death Studies*, Vol. 10(1). 1986.

Pleck, Joseph H. *The Myth of Masculinity*, Cambridge and London: MIT Press, 1981.

Pollock, G. H. "Anniversary reactions, trauma and mourning." *Psychoanalytic Quarterly*, Vol. 39, 1970.

Ramey, Estelle R. "Boredom: The Most Prevalent American Disease." *Harper's*, Nov. 1974.

Rando, Therese A. *Grief, Dying and Death*. Illinois: Research Press, 1984.

Raphael, Beverley. *The Anatomy of Bereavement*. New York: Basic Books, 1983.

Rubinstein, Robert L. "The construction of a day by elderly widowers." *International Journal of Aging and Human Development*, Vol. 23(3), 1986.

Schiff, Harriet Sarnoff. *The Bereaved Parent*. New York: Crown Publishers, Inc., 1977.

Schoenberg, Bernard, Arthur C. Carr, Austin H. Kutscher, David Peretz, and Ivan Goldberg, eds. *Anticipatory Grief*. New York: Columbia University Press, 1974.

Scully, Jean E. "Men and grieving," *Psychotherapy Patient*, Vol. 2(1) 1985.

Seligman, Martin E.P. *Helplessness*. San Francisco: W.H. Freeman and Company, 1975.

Shaffer, Martin. *Life After Stress*. New York: Plenum Press, 1982.

Shanfield, Stephen B., Andrew H. Benjamin and Barbara J. Swain. "Parent's reactions to the death of an adult child from cancer," *The American Journal of Psychiatry*, September 1984.

Shapiro, Stephen A., *Manhood*, New York: G.P. Putnam's Sons, 1984.

Shatan, Chaim F. "The grief of soldiers: Vietnam combat veteran's self-help movement." *American Journal of Orthopsychiatry*, Vol. 43 (4), 1973.

Siegal, Reva Lee, and David D. Hoefer "Bereavement counseling for gay individuals." *American Journal of Psychotherapy*, Vol. XXXV (4), October 1981.

Smith, Gudmund J.W., and Anna Danielsson. *Anxiety and Defensive Strategies in Childhood and Adolescence*. New York: International Universities Press, Inc., 1982.

Storr, Anthony. *Solitude*. New York: Ballantine Books, 1988.

Stringham, J., J.H. Riley, and A. Ross. "Silent birth: mourning a stillborn baby." Social Work, Vol. 27, 1982.

Stroebe, M.S. and W. Stroebe. "Who suffers more? Sex differences in health risks of the widowed." *Psychological Bulletin*. Vol. 93 (2), 1983.

Sulzberger, C.L. *How I Committed Suicide*, New Haven and New York: Ticknor and Fields, 1982.

Suplee, Curt. "The mystery of tears." *Smithsonian*, Vol.15 (3).

Tittensor, John. *Year One*. Australia: McPhee Gribble Publishers, 1984.

Tavris, Carol. *Anger*. New York: Simon and Schuster, 1982.

Thompson, Larry W. and Gallagher, Dolores. "Depression and its treatment in the elderly." *Aging*, U.S. Department of Health and Human Services, 1985.

Thorne, Barrie; Cheris Kramarae and Nancy Henley. *Language, Gender, and Society*. Massachusetts: Newbury House Publishers, Inc. 1983.

Thornton, Kenneth F.R.C.P.(C) "The addictive process: From the bar to the morgue." Paper presented at 29th Annual Institute on Addiction Studies, Hamilton, Ontario; July 10-15th, 1988.

Waas, Hannelore, and Charles A. Corr. *Helping Children Cope With Death*. New York: Hemisphere Publishing Corporation, 1982.

Weissman, Myrna D., and Gerald L. Klerman M.D., "Sex differences and the epidemiology of depression." *Archives of General Psychiatry*, Vol. 34, Jan 1977.

Whitfield, Charles L., M.D. *Healing The Child Within*. Florida: Health Communications, Incorporated. 1987.

Wiesel, Elie. *Against Silence*. Vol. 1. New York: Holocaust Library, 1985.

Wilson, A., J. Lawrence, D. Stevens, and D. Soule. "The death of the newborn twin: an analysis of parental bereavement." *Pediatrics*, Vol. 70, 1982.

Wistow, Fred "Goodbye." *Family Therapy Networker*, Vol.10(6) 1986.

Witherspoon, Roger "Say, Brother." *Essence*, Vol.14 (5), 1983.

Worden, William J. Grief *Counseling and Grief Therapy: A Handbook for the Mental Health Practitioner*. New York: Springer Publishing Company, 1982.

Zisook, Sidney, M.D., Stephen R. Shucter M.D., "The first four years of widowhood," *Psychiatric Annals*, Vol.16, (5), May 1986.

Other New Harbinger Self-Help Titles

I Can't Get Over It, A Handbook for Trauma Survivors, $12.95
Concerned Intervention, When Your Loved One Won't Quit Alcohol or Drugs, $11.95
Redefining Mr. Right, $11.95
Dying of Embarrassment: Help for Social Anxiety and Social Phobia, $11.95
The Depression Workbook: Living With Depression and Manic Depression, $13.95
Risk-Taking for Personal Growth: A Step-by-Step Workbook, $11.95
The Marriage Bed: Renewing Love, Friendship, Trust, and Romance, $11.95
Focal Group Psychotherapy: For Mental Health Professionals, $44.95
Hot Water Therapy: Save Your Back, Neck & Shoulders in 10 Minutes a Day $11.95
Older & Wiser: A Workbook for Coping With Aging, $12.95
Prisoners of Belief: Exposing & Changing Beliefs that Control Your Life, $10.95
Be Sick Well: A Healthy Approach to Chronic Illness, $11.95
Men & Grief: A Guide for Men Surviving the Death of a Loved One., $11.95
When the Bough Breaks: A Guide for Parents of Sexually Abused Childern, $11.95
Love Addiction: A Guide to Emotional Independence, $11.95
When Once Is Not Enough: Help for Obsessive Compulsives, $11.95
The New Three Minute Meditator, $9.95
Getting to Sleep, $10.95
The Relaxation & Stress Reduction Workbook, 3rd Edition, $13.95
Leader's Guide to the Relaxation & Stress Reduction Workbook, $19.95
Beyond Grief: A Guide for Recovering from the Death of a Loved One, $10.95
Thoughts & Feelings: The Art of Cognitive Stress Intervention, $13.95
Messages: The Communication Skills Book, $12.95
The Divorce Book, $11.95
Hypnosis for Change: A Manual of Proven Techniques, 2nd Edition, $12.95
The Deadly Diet: Recovering from Anorexia & Bulimia, $11.95
Chronic Pain Control Workbook, $13.95
Rekindling Desire: Bringing Your Sexual Relationship Back to Life, $12.95
Life Without Fear: Anxiety and Its Cure, $10.95
Visualization for Change, $12.95
Guideposts to Meaning: Discovering What Really Matters, $11.95
Videotape: Clinical Hypnosis for Stress & Anxiety Reduction, $24.95
Starting Out Right: Essential Parenting Skills for Your Child's First Seven Years, $12.95
Big Kids: A Parent's Guide to Weight Control for Children, $11.95
My Parent's Keeper: Adult Children of the Emotionally Disturbed, $11.95
When Anger Hurts, $12.95
Free of the Shadows: Recovering from Sexual Violence, $12.95
Resolving Conflict With Others and Within Yourself, $12.95
Lifetime Weight Control, $11.95
The Anxiety & Phobia Workbook, $13.95
Love and Renewal: A Couple's Guide to Commitment, $12.95
The Habit Control Workbook, $12.95

Call **toll free, 1-800-748-6273**, to order books. Have your Visa or Mastercard number ready.

Or send a check for the titles you want to New Harbinger Publications, 5674 Shattuck Avenue, Oakland, CA 94609. Include $2.00 for the first book and 50¢ for each additional book, to cover shipping and handling. (California residents please include appropriate sales tax.) Allow four to six weeks for delivery.

Prices subject to change without notice.